# TOM SLADE WITH THE BOYS OVER THERE

PERCY KEESE FITZHUGH

1st WORLD
LIBRARY
Literary Society

# Tom Slade with the Boys Over There

## Percy Keese Fitzhugh

© 1st World Library, 2006
PO Box 2211
Fairfield, IA 52556
www.1stworldlibrary.com
First Edition

LCCN: 2006907723

Softcover ISBN: 1-4218-2447-7
Hardcover ISBN: 1-4218-2347-0
eBook ISBN: 1-4218-2547-3

Purchase *"Tom Slade with the Boys Over There"*
as a traditional bound book at:
www.1stWorldLibrary.com/purchase.asp?ISBN=1-4218-2447-7

1st World Library is a literary, educational organization
dedicated to:

- Creating a free internet library of downloadable ebooks

- Hosting writing competitions and offering book
  publishing scholarships.

Interested in more 1st World Library books?
contact: literacy@1stworldlibrary.com
Check us out at: www.1stworldlibrary.com

# 1$^{st}$ World Library Literary Society

## Giving Back to the World

"If you want to work on the core problem, it's early school literacy."

**- James Barksdale, former CEO of Netscape**

"No skill is more crucial to the future of a child, or to a democratic and prosperous society, than literacy."

**- Los Angeles Times**

Literacy... means far more than learning how to read and write... The aim is to transmit... knowledge and promote social participation."

**- UNESCO**

"Literacy is not a luxury, it is a right and a responsibility. If our world is to meet the challenges of the twenty-first century we must harness the energy and creativity of all our citizens."

**- President Bill Clinton**

"Parents should be encouraged to read to their children, and teachers should be equipped with all available techniques for teaching literacy, so the varying needs and capacities of individual kids can be taken into account."

**- Hugh Mackay**

To

F. A. O.

The real Tom Slade, whose extraordinary adventures on land and sea put these storied exploits in the shade, this book is dedicated with envious admiration.

# CONTENTS

# CHAPTER I

## THE HOME IN ALSACE

In the southwestern corner of the domains of Kaiser Bill, in a fair district to which he has no more right than a highwayman has to his victim's wallet, there is a quaint old house built of gray stone and covered with a clinging vine.

In the good old days when Alsace was a part of France the old house stood there and was the scene of joy and plenty. In these evil days when Alsace belongs to Kaiser Bill, it stands there, its dim arbor and pretty, flower-laden trellises in strange contrast to the lumbering army wagons and ugly, threatening artillery which pass along the quiet road.

And if the prayers of its rightful owners are answered, it will still stand there in the happy days to come when fair Alsace shall be a part of France again and Kaiser Bill and all his clanking claptrap are gone from it forever.

The village in which this pleasant homestead stands is close up under the boundary of Rhenish Bavaria, or Germany proper (or improper), and in the happy days when Alsace was a part of France it had been known as Leteur, after the French family which for generations had lived in the old gray house.

But long before Kaiser Bill knocked down Rheims Cathedral and black-jacked Belgium and sank the Lusitania, he changed the name of this old French village to Dundgardt, showing that even then he believed in Frightfulness; for that is what it amounted to when he changed Leteur to Dundgardt.

But he could not very well change the old family name, even if he could change the names of towns and villages in his stolen province, and old Pierre Leteur and his wife and daughter lived in the old house under the Prussian menace, and managed the vineyard and talked French on the sly.

On a certain fair evening old Pierre and his wife and daughter sat in the arbor and chatted in the language which they loved. The old man had lost an arm in the fighting when his beloved Alsace was lost to France and he had come back here still young but crippled and broken-hearted, to live under the Germans because this was the home of his people. He had found the old house and the vineyard devastated.

After a while he married an Alsatian girl very much younger than himself, and their son and daughter had grown up, German subjects it is true, but hating their German masters and loving the old French Alsace of which their father so often told them.

While Florette was still a mere child she committed the heinous crime of singing the *Marseillaise.* The watchful Prussian authorities learned of this and a couple of Prussian soldiers came after her, for she must answer to the Kaiser for this terrible act of sedition.

Her brother Armand, then a boy of sixteen, had shouted "*Vive la France!*" in the very faces of the grim soldiers and had struck one of them with all his young strength.

In that blow spoke gallant, indomitable France!

For this act Armand might have been shot, but, being young and agile and the German soldiers being fat and clumsy, he effected a flank move and disappeared before they could lay hands on him and it was many a long day before ever his parents heard from him again.

At last there came a letter from far-off America, telling of his flight across the mountains into France and of his working his passage to the United States. How this letter got through the Prussian censorship against all French Alsatians, it would be hard to say. But it was the first and last word from him that had ever reached the blighted home.

After a while the storm cloud of the great war burst and then the prospect of hearing from Armand became more hopeless as the British navy threw its mighty arm across the ocean highway. And old Pierre, because he was a French veteran, was watched more suspiciously than ever.

Florette was nearly twenty now, and Armand must be twenty-three or four, and they were talking of him on this quiet, balmy night, as they sat together in the arbor. They spoke in low tones, for to talk in French was dangerous, they were already under the cloud of suspicion, and the very trees in the neighborhood of a Frenchman's home seemed to have ears....

# CHAPTER II

## AN APPARITION

"But how could we hear from him now, Florette, any better than before?" the old man asked.

"America is our friend now," the girl answered, "and so good things must happen."

"Indeed, great things will happen, dear Florette," her father laughed, "and our beloved Alsace will be restored and you shall sing the *Marseillaise* again. *Vive l'Amerique!* She has come to us at last!"

"Sh-h-h," warned Madame Leteur, looking about; "because America has joined us is no reason we should not be careful. See how our neighbor Le Farge fared for speaking in the village but yesterday. It is glorious news, but we must be careful."

"What did neighbor Le Farge say, mamma?"

"Sh-h-h. The news of it is not allowed. He said that some one told him that when the American General Pershing came to France, he stood by the grave of Lafayette and said, 'Lafayette, we are here.'"

"Ah, Lafayette, yes!" said the old man, his voice shaking with pride.

"But we must not even know there is a great army of Americans here. We must know nothing. We must be blind and deaf," said Madame Leteur, looking about her apprehensively.

"America will bring us many good things, my sweet Florette," said her father more cautiously, "and she will bring triumph to our gallant France. But we must have patience. How can she send us letters from Armand, my dear? How can she send letters to Germany, her enemy?"

"Then we shall never hear of him till the war is over?" the girl sighed. "Oh, it is my fault he went away! It was my heedless song and I cannot forgive myself."

"The *Marseillaise* is not a heedless song, Florette," said old Pierre, "and when our brave boy struck the Prussian beast -"

"Sh-h-h," whispered Madame Leteur quickly.

"There is no one," said the old man, peering cautiously into the bushes; "when he struck the Prussian beast, it was only what his father's son must do. Come, cheer up! Think of those noble words of America's general, 'Lafayette, we are here.' If we have not letters from our son, still America has come to us. Is not this enough? She will strike the Prussian beast -"

"Sh-h-h!"

"There is no one, I tell you. She will strike the Prussian beast with her mighty arm harder than our poor noble boy could do with his young hand. Is it not so?"

The girl looked wistfully into the dusk. "I thought we would hear from him when we had the great news from America."

"That is because you are a silly child, my sweet Florette, and think that America is a magician. We must be patient. We do not even know all that her great president said. We are fed with lies -"

"Sh-h-h!"

"And how can we hear from Armand, my dear, when the Prussians do not even let us know what America's president said? All will be well in good time."

"He is dead," said the girl, uncomforted. "I have had a dream that he is dead. And it is I that killed him."

"This is a silly child," said old Pierre.

"America is full of Prussians - spies," said the girl, "and they have his name on a list. They have killed him. They are murderers!"

"Sh-h-h," warned her mother again.

"Yes, they are murderers," said old Pierre, "but this is a silly child to talk so. We have borne much silently. Can we not be a little patient now?"

"I *hate* them!" sobbed the girl, abandoning all caution. "They drove him away and we will see him no more, - my brother - Armand!"

"Hush, my daughter," her mother pleaded. "Listen! I heard a footstep. They are spying and have heard."

For a moment neither spoke and there was no sound but the girl's quick breaths as she tried to control herself. Then there was a slight rustling in the shrubbery and they waited in breathless suspense.

"I knew it," whispered Madame; "we are always watched. Now it has come."

Still they waited, fearfully. Another sound, and old Pierre rose, pushed his rustic chair from him and stood with a fine, soldierly air, waiting. His wife was trembling pitiably and Florette, her eyes wide with grief and terror, watched the dark bushes like a frightened animal.

Suddenly the leaves parted and they saw a strange disheveled figure. For a moment it paused, uncertain, then looked stealthily about and emerged into the open. The stranger was hatless and barefoot and his whole appearance was that of exhaustion and fright. When he spoke it was in a strange language and spasmodically as if he had been running hard.

"Leteur?" he asked, looking from one to the other; "the name - Leteur? I can't speak French," he added, somewhat bewildered and clutching an upright of the arbor.

"What do you wish here?" old Pierre demanded in French, never relaxing his military air.

The stranger leaned wearily against the arbor, panting, and even in the dusk they could see that he was young and very ragged, and with the whiteness of fear and apprehension in his face and his staring eyes.

"You German? French?" he panted.

"We are French," said Florette, rising. "I can speak ze Anglaise a leetle."

"You are not German?" the visitor repeated as if relieved.

"Only we are Zherman subjects, yess. Our name ees Leteur."

"I am - American. My name - is Tom Slade. I escaped from the prison across there. My - my pal escaped with me -"

The girl looked pityingly at him and shook her head while her parents listened curiously. "We are sorry," she said, "so sorry; but you were not wise to escape. We cannot shelter you. We are suspect already."

"I have brought you news of Armand," said Tom. "I can't - can't talk. We ran - Here, take this. He - he gave it to me - on the ship."

He handed Florette a little iron button, which she took with a trembling hand, watching him as he clutched the arbor post.

"From Armand? You know heem?" she asked, amazed. "You are American?"

"He's American, too," said Tom, "and he's with General Pershing in France. We're goin' to join him if you'll help us."

For a moment the girl stared straight at him, then turning to her father she poured out such a volley of French as would have staggered the grim authorities of poor Alsace. What she said the fugitive could not imagine, but presently old Pierre stepped forward and, throwing his one arm about the neck of the young American, kissed him several times with great fervor.

Tom Slade was not used to being kissed by anybody and he was greatly abashed. However, it might have been worse. What would he ever have done if the girl who spoke English in such a hesitating, pretty way had taken it into *her* head to kiss him?

# CHAPTER III

## TOM'S STORY

"You needn't be afraid," said Tom; "we didn't leave any tracks; we came across the fields - all the way from the crossroads down there. We crawled along the fence. There ain't any tracks. I looked out for that."

Pausing in suspense, yet encouraged by their expectant silence, he spoke to some one behind him in the bushes and there emerged a young fellow quite as ragged as himself.

"It's all right," said Tom confidently, and apparently in great relief. "It's them."

"You must come inside ze house," whispered Florette fearfully. "It is not safe to talk here."

"There isn't any one following us," said Tom's companion reassuringly. "If we can just get some old clothes and some grub we'll be all right."

"Zere is much danger," said the girl, unconvinced. "We are always watched. But you are friends to Armand. We must help you."

She led the way into the house and into a simply furnished room lighted by a single lamp and as she cautiously shut the heavy wooden blinds and lowered the light, the two fugitives looked eagerly at the first signs of home life which they had seen in many a long day.

It was in vain that the two Americans declined the wine which old Pierre insisted upon their drinking.

"You will drink zhust a leetle - yess?" said the girl prettily. "It is make in our own veenyard."

So the boys sipped a little of the wine and found it grateful to their weary bodies and overwrought nerves.

"Now you can tell us - of Armand," she said eagerly.

Often during Tom's simple story she stole to the window and, opening the blind slightly, looked fearfully along the dark, quiet road. The very atmosphere of the room seemed charged with nervous apprehension and every sound of the breeze without startled the tense nerves of the little party.

Old Pierre and his wife, though quite unable to understand, listened keenly to every word uttered by the strangers, interrupting their daughter continually to make her translate this or that sentence.

"There ain't so much need to worry," said Tom, with a kind of dogged self-confidence that relieved Florette not a little. "I wouldn't of headed for here if I hadn't known I could do it without leaving any trace, 'cause I wouldn't want to get you into trouble."

Florette looked intently at the square, dull face before her with its big mouth and its suggestion of a frown. His shock of hair, always rebellious, was now in utter disorder. He was barefoot and his clothes were in that condition which only the neglect and squalor of a German prison camp can produce. But in his gaunt face there shone a look of determination and a some-thing which seemed to encourage the girl to believe in him.

Percy Keese Fitzhugh

"Are zey all like you - ze Americans?" she asked.

"Some of 'em are taller than me," he answered literally, "but I got a good chest expansion. This feller's name is Archer. He belongs on a farm in New York."

She glanced at Archer and saw a round, red, merry face, still wearing that happy-go-lucky look which there is no mistaking. His skin was camouflaged by a generous coat of tan and those two strategic hills, his cheeks, had not been reduced by the assaults of hunger. There was, moreover, a look of mischief in his eyes, bespeaking a jaunty acceptance of whatever peril and adventure might befall and when he spoke he rolled his R's and screwed up his mouth accordingly.

"Maybe you've heard of the Catskills," said Tom. "That's where *he* lives."

"My dad's got a big apple orrcharrd therre," added Archer.

Florette Leteur had not heard of the Catskills, but she had heard a good deal about the Americans lately and she looked from one to the other of this hapless pair, who seemed almost to have dropped from the clouds.

"You have been not wise to escape," she said sympathetically. "Ze Prussians, zey are sure to catch you. - Tell me more of my bruzzer."

"The Prussians ain't so smarrt," said Archer. "They're good at some things, but when it comes to tracking and trailing and all that, they're no good. You neverr hearrd of any famous Gerrman scouts. They're clumsy. They couldn't stalk a mud turrtle."

"You are not afraid of zem?"

"Surre, we ain't. Didn't we just put one overr on 'em?"

"We looped our trail," explained Tom to the puzzled girl. "If they're after us at all they probably went north on a blind trail. We monkeyed the trees all the way through this woods near here."

"He means we didn't touch the ground," explained Archer.

"We made seven footprints getting across the road to the fence and then we washed 'em away by chucking sticks. And, anyway, we crossed the road backwards so they'd think we were going the other way. There ain't much danger - not tonight, anyway."

Again the girl looked from one to the other and then explained to her father as best she could.

"You are wonderful," she said simply. "We shall win ze war now."

"I was working as a mess boy on a transport," said Tom; "we brought over about five thousand soldiers. That's how I got acquainted with Frenchy - I mean Armand -"

"Yes!" she cried, and at the mention of Armand old Pierre could scarcely keep his seat.

"He came with some soldiers from Illinois. That's out west. He was good-natured and all the soldiers jollied him. But he always said he didn't mind that because they were all going to fight together to get Alsace back. Jollying means making fun of somebody - kind of," Tom added.

"Oh, zat iss what he say?" Florette cried. "Zat iss my brother - Armand - yess!"

She explained to her parents and then advanced upon Tom, who retreated to his second line of defence behind a chair to save himself from the awful peril of a grateful caress.

"He told me all about how your father fought in the Franco-Prussian War," Tom went on, "and he gave me this button and he said it was made from a cannon they used and -"

"Ah, yess, I know!" Florette exclaimed delightedly.

"He said if I should ever happen to be in Alsace all I'd have to do would be to show it to any French people and they'd help me. He said it was a kind of - a kind of a vow all the French people had - that the Germans didn't know anything about. And 'specially families that had men in the Franco-Prussian War. He told me how he escaped, too, and got to America, and about how he hit the German soldier that came to arrest you for singing the *Marseillaise*."

The girl's face colored with anger, and yet with pride.

"Mostly what we came here for," Tom added in his expressionless way, "was to get some food and get rested before we start again. We're going through Switzerland to join the Americans - and if you'll wait a little while you can sing the *Marseillaise* all you want."

Something in his look and manner as he sat there, uncouth and forlorn, sent a thrill through her.

"Zey are all like you?" she repeated. "Ze Americans?"

"Your brother and I got to be pretty good friends," said Tom simply; "he talked just like you. When we got to a French port - I ain't allowed to tell you the name of it - but when we got there he went away on the train with all the other soldiers, and he waved his hand to me and said he was going to win Alsace back. I liked him and I liked the way he talked. He got excited, like -"

"Ah, yess - my bruzzer!"

"So now he's with General Pershing. It seemed funny not to

see him after that. I thought about him a lot. When he talked it made me feel more patriotic and proud, like."

"Yess, yess," she urged, the tears standing in her eyes.

"Sometimes you sort of get to like a feller and you don't know why. He would always get so excited, sort of, when he talked about France or Uncle Sam that he'd throw his cigarette away. He wasted a lot of 'em. He said everybody's got two countries, his own and France."

"Ah, yess," she exclaimed.

"Even if I didn't care anything about the war," Tom went on in his dull way, "I'd want to see France get Alsace back just on account of him."

Florette sat gazing at him, her eyes brimming.

"And you come to Zhermany, how?"

"After we started back the ship I worked on got torpedoed and I was picked up by a submarine. I never saw the inside of one before. So that's how I got to Germany. They took me there and put me in the prison camp at Slopsgotten - that ain't the way to say it, but -"

"You've got to sneeze it," interrupted Archer.

"Yes, I know," she urged eagerly, "and zen -"

"And then when I found out that it was just across the border from Alsace I happened to think about having that button, and I thought if I could escape maybe the French people would help me if I showed it to 'em like Frenchy said."

"Oh, yess, *zey will!* But we must be careful," said Florette.

"It was funny how I met Archer there," said Tom. "We used to

Percy Keese Fitzhugh

know each other in New York. He had even more adventures than I did getting there."

"And you escaped?"

"Yop."

"We put one over on 'em," said Archer. "It was his idea (indicating Tom). They let us have some chemical stuff to fix the pump engine with and we melted the barbed wire with it and made a place to crawl out through. I got a piece of the barbed wirre for a sooveneerr. Maybe you'd like to have it," Archer added, fumbling in his pockets.

Florette, smiling and crying all at once, still sat looking wonderingly from one to the other of this adventurous, ragged pair.

"Those Germans ain't so smart," said Archer.

The girl only shook her head and explained to her parents. Then she turned to Tom.

"My father wants to know if zey are all like you in America. Yess?"

"*He* used to be a Boy Scout," said Archer. "Did you everr hearr of them?"

But Florette only shook her head again and stared. Ever since the war began she had lived under the shadow of the big prison camp. Many of her friends and townspeople, Alsatians loyal still to France, were held there among the growing horde of foreigners. Never had she heard of any one escaping. If two American boys could melt the wires and walk out, what would happen next?

And one of them had blithely announced that these mighty invincible Prussians "couldn't even trail a mud turtle." She wondered what they meant by "looping our trail."

## CHAPTER IV

## THE OLD WINE VAT

"We thought maybe you'd let us stay here tonight and tomorrow," said Tom after the scanty meal which the depleted larder yielded, "and tomorrow night we'll start out south; 'cause we don't want to be traveling in the daytime. Maybe you could give us some clothes so it'll change our looks. It's less than a hundred miles to Basel -"

"My pappa say you could nevaire cross ze frontier. Zere are wires - electric -"

"Electric wirres are ourr middle name," said Archer. "We eat 'em."

"We ain't scared of anything except the daylight," said Tom. "Archy can talk some German and I got Frenchy's - Armand's - button to show to French people. When we once get into Switzerland we'll be all right."

He waited while the girl engaged in an animated talk with her parents. Then old Pierre patted the two boys affectionately on the shoulder while Florette explained.

"It iss not for our sake only, it iss for yours. You cannot stay in ziss house. It iss not safe. You aire wonderful, zee how you escape, and to bring us news of our Armand! We must help you. But if zey get you zen we do not help you. Iss it so? Here

Percy Keese Fitzhugh

every day ze Prussians come. You see? Zey do not follow you - you are what you say - too clevaire? But still zey come."

Tom listened, his heart in his throat at the thought of being turned out of this home where he had hoped for shelter.

"We are already suspect," Florette explained. "My pappa, he fought for France - long ago. But so zey hate him. My name zey get - how old - All zeze zings zey write down - everyzing. Zey come for me soon. I sang ze *Marseillaise* - you know?"

"Yes," said Tom, "but that was years ago."

"But we are suspect. Zey have write it all down. Nossing zey forget. Zey take me to work - out of Alsace. Maybe to ze great Krupps. I haf to work in ze fields in Prussia maybe. You see? Ven zey come I must go. Tonight, maybe. Tomorrow. Maybe not yet -"

She struggled to master her emotion and continued. "Ziss is - what you call - blackleest house. You see? So you will hide where I take you. It iss bad, but we cannot help. I give you food and tomorrow in ze night I bring you clothes. Zese I must look for - Armand's. You see? Come."

They rose with her and as she stood there almost overcome with grief and shame and the strain of long suspense and apprehension, yet thinking only of their safety, the sadness of her position and her impending fate went to Tom's heart.

Old Pierre embraced the boys affectionately with his one arm, seeming to confirm all his daughter had said.

"My pappa say it is best you stay not here in ziss house. I will show you where Armand used to hide so long ago when we play," she smiled through her tears. "If zey come and find you -"

"I understand," said Tom. "They couldn't blame it to you."

"You see? Yess."

To Archer, who understood a few odds and ends of German old Pierre managed to explain in that language his sorrow and humiliation at their poor welcome.

All five then went into an old-fashioned kitchen with walls of naked masonry and a great chimney, and from a cupboard Florette and her mother filled a basket with such cold viands as were on hand. This, and a pail of water the boys carried, and after another affectionate farewell from Pierre and his wife, they followed the girl cautiously and silently out into the darkness.

Tom Slade had already felt the fangs of the German beast and he did not need any one to tell him that the loathsome thing was without conscience or honor, but as he watched the slender form of Armand's young sister hurrying on ahead of them and thought of all she had borne and must yet bear and of the black fear that must be always in her young heart, his sympathy for her and for this stricken home was very great.

He had not fully comprehended her meaning, but he understood that she and her parents were haunted by an ever-present dread, and that even in their apprehension it hurt them to skimp their hospitality or suffer any shadow to be cast on a stranger's welcome.

Florette led the way along a narrow board path running back from the house, through an endless maze of vine-covered arbor, which completely roofed all the grounds adjacent to the house. Tom, accustomed only to the small American grape arbor, was amazed at the extent of this vineyard.

"Reminds you of an elevated railroad, don't it," said Archer.

On the rickety uprights (for the arbor like everything else on the old place was going to ruin under the alien blight) large baskets hung here and there. At intervals the structure sagged so that they had to stoop to pass under it, and here and there it was broken or uncovered and they caught glimpses of the sky.

They went over a little hillock and, still beneath the arbor, came upon a place where the vines had fallen away from the ramshackle trellis and formed a spreading mass upon the ground.

"You see?" whispered the girl in her pretty way. "Here Armand he climb. Here he hide to drop ze grapes down my neck - so. Bad boy! So zen it break - crash! He tumbled down. Ah - my pappa so angry. We must nevaire climb on ze trellis. You see? Here I sit and laugh - so much - when he tumble down!"

She smiled and for a moment seemed all happiness, but Tom Slade heard a sigh following close upon the smile. He did not know what to say so he simply said in his blunt way:

"I guess you had good times together."

"Now I will zhow you," she said, stooping to pull away the heavy tangle of vine.

Tom and Archer helped her and to their surprise there was revealed a trap-door about six feet in diameter with gigantic rusty hinges.

"Ziss is ze cave - you see?" she said, stooping to lift the door. Tom bent but she held him back. "Wait, I will tell you. Zen you can open it." For a moment pleasant recollections seemed to have the upper hand, and there was about her a touch of that buoyancy which had made her brother so attractive to sober Tom.

"Wait - zhest till I tell you. When I come back from ze school in England I have read ze story about 'Kidnap.' You know?"

"It's by Stevenson; I read it," said Archer.

"You know ze cave vere ze Scotch man live? So ziss is our cave. Now you lift."

The door did not stir at first and Florette, laughing softly, raised the big L band which bent over the top and lay in a rusted padlock eye.

"Now."

The boys raised the heavy door, to which many strands of the vine clung, and Florette placed a stick to hold it up at an angle. Peering within by the light of a match, they saw the interior of what appeared to be a mammoth hogshead from which emanated a stale, but pungent odor. It was, perhaps, seven feet in depth and the same in diameter and the bottom was covered with straw.

"It is ze vat - ze wine vat," whispered Florette, amused at their surprise. "Here we keep ze wine zat will cost so much. - But no more. - We make no wine ziss year," she sighed. "Ziss makes ze fine flavor - ze earth all around. You see?"

"It's a dandy place to hide," said Archer.

"So here you will stay and you will be safe. Tomorrow in ze night I shall bring you more food and some clothes. I am so sorry -"

"There ain't anything to be sorry about," said Tom. "There's lots of room in there - more than there is in a bivouac tent. And it'll be comfortable on that straw, that's one sure thing. If you knew the kind of place we slept in up there in the prison you'd say this was all right. We'll stay here and rest all day tomorrow and after you bring us the things at night we'll sneak out and hike it along."

"I will not dare to come in ze daytime," said Florette, "but after it is dark, zen I will come. You must have ze cover almost shut and I will pull ze vines over it."

"We'll tend to that," said Tom.

"We'll camouflage it, all right," Archer added.

For a moment she lingered as if thinking if there were anything more she might do for their comfort. Then against her protest, Tom accompanied her part way back and they paused for a moment under the thickly covered trellis, for she would not let him approach the house.

"I'm sorry we made you so much trouble," he said; "it's only because we want to get to where we can fight for you."

"Oh, yess, I know," she answered sadly. "My pappa, it break his heart because he cannot make you ze true welcome. But you do not know. We are - how you say - persecute - all ze time. Zey own Alsace, but zey do not love Alsace. It is like - it is like ze stepfather - you see?" she added, her voice breaking. "So zey have always treat us."

For a few seconds Tom stood, awkward and uncomfortable; then clumsily he reached out his hand and took hers.

"You don't mean they'll take you like they took the people from Belgium, do you?" he asked.

"Ziss is worse zan Belgium," Florette sobbed. "Zere ze people can escape to England."

"Where would they send you?" Tom asked.

"Maybe far north into Prussia. Maybe still in Alsace. All ze familees zey will separate so zey shall meex wiz ze Zhermans." Florette suddenly grasped his hand. "I am glad I see you. So now I can see all ze Americans come - hoondreds -

"Tomorrow in ze night I will bring you ze clothes," she whispered, "and more food, and zen you will be rested -"

"I feel sorry for you," Tom blurted out with simple honesty, "and I got to thank you. Both of us have - that's one sure thing. You're worse off than we are - and it makes me feel mean, like. But maybe it won't be so bad. And, gee, I'll look forward to seeing you tomorrow night, too."

"I will bring ze sings, *surely*," she said earnestly.

"It isn't - it isn't only for that," he mumbled, "it's because I'll kind of look forward to seeing you anyway."

For another moment she lingered and in the stillness of night and the thickly roofed arbor he could hear her breath coming short and quick, as she tried to stifle her emotion.

"Is - is it a sound?" she whispered in sudden terror.

"No, it's only because you're scared," said Tom.

He stood looking after her as she hurried away under the ramshackle trellis until her slender figure was lost in the darkness.

"It'll make me fight harder, anyway," he said to himself; "it'll help me to get to France 'cause - 'cause I *got* to, and if you *got* to do a thing - you can...."

# CHAPTER V

## THE VOICE FROM THE DISTANCE

"My idea," said Archer, when Tom returned, "is to break that stick about in half and prop the doorr just wide enough open so's we can crawl in. Then we can spread the vines all overr the top just like it was beforre and overr the opening, too. What d'ye say?"

"That's all right," said Tom, "and we can leave it a little open tonight. In the morning we'll drop it and be on the safe side."

"Maybe we'd betterr drop it tonight and be on the safe side," said Archer. "S'pose we should fall asleep."

"We'll take turns sleeping," said Tom decisively. "We can't afford to take any chances."

"You can bet I'm going to get a sooveneerr of this place, anyway," said Archer, tugging at a rusty nail.

"Never you mind about souvenirs," Tom said; "let's get this door camouflaged."

"I could swap that nail for a jack-knife back home," said Archer regretfully. "A nail right fresh from Alsace!"

But he gave it up and together they pulled the tangled vine this way and that, until the door and the opening beneath were well covered. Then they crawled in and while Archer reached up and held the door, Tom broke the stick so that the opening was reduced to the inch or two necessary for ventilation. Reaching out, they pulled the vine over this crack until they felt certain that no vestige of door or opening could be seen from without, and this done they sat down upon the straw, their backs against the walls of the vat, enjoying the first real comfort and freedom from anxiety which they had known since their escape from the prison camp.

"I guess we're safe herre forr tonight, anyway," said Archer, "but believe *me*, I think we've got some job on our hands getting out of this country. It's going to be no churrch sociable -"

"We got this far," said Tom, "and by tomorrow night we ought to have a good plan doped out. We got nothing to do all day tomorrow but think about it."

"Gee, I feel sorry for these people," said Archer; "they'rre surre up against it. Makes me feel as if I'd like to have one good whack at Kaiser Bill -"

"Well, don't talk so loud and we'll get a whack at him, all right."

"I'd like to get his old double-jointed moustache for a sooveneerr."

"There you go again," said Tom.

Now that the excitement was over, they realized how tired they were and indeed the strain upon their nerves, added to their bodily fatigue, had brought them almost to the point of exhaustion.

"I'm all in," said Archer wearily.

"All right, go to sleep," said Tom, "and after a while if you don't wake up I'll wake you. One of us has got to stay awake and listen. We can't afford to take any chances."

Archibald Archer needed no urging and in a minute he was sprawled upon the straw, dead to the world. The daylight was glinting cheerily through the interstices of tangled vine over the opening when he awoke with the heedless yawns which he might have given in his own beloved Catskills.

"Don't make a noise," said Tom quickly, by way of caution. "We're in the wine vat in Leteur's vineyard in Alsace, remember." It took Archer a moment to realize where they were. They ate an early breakfast, finding the simple odds and ends grateful enough, and then Tom took his turn at a nap.

Throughout most of that day they sat with their knees drawn up, leaning against the inside of the great vat, talking in hushed tones of their plans. There was nothing else they could do in the half darkness and the slow hours dragged themselves away monotonously. They had lowered the door, but still left it open upon the merest crack and out of this one or the other would peek at intervals, listening, heart in throat, for the dreaded sound of footfalls. But no one came.

"I thought I hearrd a kind of rustling once," Archer said fearfully.

"There's a couple of cows 'way over in a field," said Tom; "they might have made some sound."

After what seemed to them an age, the leaves over the opening seemed bathed in a strange new light and glistened here and there.

"That crack faces the west," said Tom. "The sun's beginning to go down."

"How do you know?" asked Archer.

"I always knew that up at Temple Camp. I don't know *how*

I know. The morning sun is different from the afternoon sun, that's all. I think it'll set now in about two hours."

"I wonder when she'll come," Archer said.

"Not till it's good and dark, that's sure. She's got to be careful. Maybe this place can be seen from the road, for all we know. Remember, we didn't see it in the daylight."

"Sh-h-h," said Archer. "Listen."

From far, far away there was borne upon the still air a dull, spent, booming sound at intervals.

"It's the fighting," whispered Tom.

"Wherre do you suppose it is?" Archer asked, sobered by this audible reminder of their nearness to the seat of war.

"I don't know," Tom said. "I'm kind of mixed up. That feller in the prison had a map. Let's see. I think Nancy's the nearest place to here. Toul is near that. That's where our fellers are - around there. Listen!"

Again the rumbling, faint but distinctly audible, almost as if it came from another world.

"The trenches run right through there - near Nancy," said Tom.

"Maybe it's *ourr* boys, hey?" Archer asked excitedly.

Tom did not answer immediately. He was thrilled at this thought of his own country speaking so that he, poor fugitive that he was, could hear it in this dark, lonesome dungeon in a hostile land, across all those miles.

"Maybe," he said, his voice catching the least bit. "They're in the Toul sector. A feller in prison told me. You don't feel so

Percy Keese Fitzhugh

lonesome, kind of, when you hear that -"

"Gee, I hope we can get to them," said Archer.

"What you *got* to do, you can do," Tom answered. "I wonder -"

"Sh-h. D'you hearr that?" Archer whispered, clutching Tom's shoulder. "It was much nearerr - right close -"

They held their breaths as the reverberation of a sharp report died away.

"What was it?" Archer asked tensely.

"I don't know," Tom whispered, instinctively removing the short stick and closing the trap door tight. "Don't move - hush!"

# CHAPTER VI

## PRISONERS AGAIN

"Do you hear footsteps?" Archer breathed.

Tom listened, keen and alert. "No," he said at last. "There's no one coming."

"What do you s'pose it was?"

"I don't know. Sit down and don't get excited."

But Tom was trembling himself, and it was not until five or ten minutes had passed without sound or happening that he was able to get a grip on himself.

"Push up the door a little and listen," suggested Archer.

Tom cautiously pressed upward, but the door did not budge. "It's stuck," he whispered.

Archer rose and together they pressed, but save for a little looseness the door did not move.

"It's caught outside, I guess," said Tom. "Maybe the iron hasp fell into the padlock when I put it down, huh?"

That, indeed, seemed to be the case, for upon pressure the door gave a little at the corners, but not midway along the side

Percy Keese Fitzhugh

where the fastening was. Archer turned cold at the thought of their predicament, and for a moment even Tom's rather dull imagination pictured the ghastly fate made possible by imprisonment in this black hole.

"There's no use getting excited," he said. "We get some air through the cracks and after dark she'll be here, like she said. It's beginning to get dark now, I guess."

But he could not sit quietly and wait through the awful suspense, and he pressed up against the boards at intervals all the way along the four sides of the door. On the side where the hinges were it yielded not at all. On the opposite side it held fast in the center, showing that by a perverse freak of chance it had locked itself. Elsewhere it strained a little on pressure, but not enough to afford any hope of breaking it.

"If it was only lowerr," Archer said, "so we could brace our shoulderrs against it, we might forrce it."

"And make a lot of noise," said Tom. "There's no use getting rattled; we'll just have to wait till she comes."

"Yes, but it gives you the willies thinkin' about what would happen -"

"Well, don't let's think of it, then," Tom interrupted. "We should worry." And suiting his action to the word, he seated himself, drew up his knees, and clasped his hands over them. "We'll just have to wait, that's all."

"What do you suppose that sound was?" Archer asked.

"I don't know; some kind of a gun. It ain't the first gun that's been shot off in Europe lately."

For half an hour or so they sat, trying to make talk, and each pretended to himself and to the other that he was not worrying. But Tom, who had a scout's ear, started and his heart beat faster at every trifling stir outside. Then, as they realized that darkness must have fallen, they became more alert for sounds and a little apprehensive. They knew Florette would come quietly, but Tom believed he could detect her approach.

After a while, they abandoned all their pretence of nonchalant confidence and did not talk at all. Of course, they knew Florette would come in her own good time, but the stifling atmosphere of that musty hole and the thought of what *might* happen -

Suddenly there was a slight noise outside and then, to their great relief, the unmistakable sound of footfalls on the planks above them, softened by the thick carpet of matted vine.

"Sh-h, don't speak!" Tom whispered, his heart beating rapidly. "Wait till she unfastens it or says something."

For a few seconds - a minute - they waited in breathless suspense. Then came a slight rustle as from some disturbance of the vine, then footfalls, again, modulated and stealthy they seemed, on the door just above them. A speck of dirt, or an infinitesimal pebble, maybe, fell upon Archer's head from the slight jarring of some crack in the rough door. Then silence.

Breathlessly they waited, Archer nervously clutching Tom's arm.

"Don't speak," Tom warned in the faintest whisper.

Still they waited. But no other sound broke upon the deathlike solitude and darkness....

Percy Keese Fitzhugh

# CHAPTER VII

## WHERE THERE'S A WILL ----

"They're hunting for us," whispered Tom hoarsely. "It's good it was shut."

"I'd ratherr have them catch us," shivered Archer, "than die in herre."

"We haven't died yet," said Tom, "and they haven't caught us either. Don't lose your nerves. She'll come as soon as she can."

For a few minutes they did not speak nor stir, only listened eagerly for any further sound.

"What do you s'pose that shot was?" Archer whispered, after a few minutes more of keen suspense.

"I don't know. A signal, maybe. They're searching this place for us, I guess. Don't talk."

Archer took comfort from Tom's calmness, and for half an hour more they waited, silent and apprehensive. But nothing more happened, the solemn stillness of the countryside reigned without, and as the time passed their fear of pursuit and capture gave way to cold terror at the thought of being locked in this black, stifling vault to die.

What had happened? What did that shot mean, and where was it? Why did Florette not come? Who had walked across the plank roof of that musty prison? The fact that they could only guess at the time increased their dread and made their dreadful predicament the harder to bear. Moreover, the air was stale and insufficient and their heads began to ache cruelly.

"We can't stand it in here much longer," Tom confessed, after what seemed a long period of waiting. "Pretty soon one of us will be all in and then it'll be harder for the other. We've got to get out, no matter what."

"Therre may be a Gerrman soldierr within ten feet of us now," Archer said. "They'rre probably around in this vineyarrd *somewherre*, anyway. If we tried to forrce it open they'd hearr us."

"We couldn't force it, anyway," Tom said.

"My head's pounding like a hammerr," said Archer after a few minutes more of silence.

"Hold some of that damp straw to it. - How many matches did she give you?"

"'Bout a dozen or so."

"Wish I had a knife. - Have you got that piece of wire yet?"

"Surre I have," said Archer, hauling from his pocket about five inches of barbed wire - the treasured memento of his escape from the Hun prison camp. "You laughed at me for always gettin' sooveneerrs; now you see - What you want it for?"

"Sh-h. How many barbs has it?" asked Tom in a cautious whisper.

"Three."

"Let's have it; give me a couple o' matches, too."

Holding a lighted match under the place where he thought the iron padlock band must be, he scrutinized the under side of the door for any sign of it.

"I thought maybe the ends of the screws would show through," he said.

"What's the idea?" Archer asked. "Gee, but my head's poundin'."

"If that hasp just fell over the padlock eye," Tom whispered, "and didn't fit in like it ought to, maybe if I could bore a hole right under it I could push it up. Don't get scared," he added impassively. "There's another way, too; but it's a lot of work and it would make a noise. We'd just have to settle down and take turns and dig through with the wire barbs. I wish we had more matches. Don't get rattled, now. I know we're in a dickens of a hole -"

"You said something," observed Archer.

"I didn't mean it for a joke," said Tom soberly.

"This has got the trenches beat a mile," Archer said, somewhat encouraged by Tom's calmness and resourcefulness.

Striking another match, Tom examined more carefully the area of planking just in the middle of the side where he knew the hasp must be. He determined the exact center as nearly as he could. While doing this he dug his fingernails under a large splinter in the old planking and pulled it loose. Archer could not see what he was doing, and something deterred him from bothering his companion with questions.

For a while Tom breathed heavily on the splintered fragment. Then he tore one end of it until it was in shreds.

"Let's have another match."

Igniting the shredded end, he blew it deftly until the solid wood was aflame, and by the light of it he could see that Archer was ghastly pale and almost on the point of collapse. Their dank, unwholesome refuge seemed the more dreadful for the light.

"You got to just think about our getting out," Tom said, in his usual dull manner. "We won't suffocate near so soon if we don't think about it, and don't get rattled. We *got* to get out and so we *will* get out. Let's have that wire."

All Archer's buoyancy was gone, but he tried to take heart from his comrade's stolid, frowning face and quiet demeanor.

"We can set fire to the whole business if we have to," said Tom, "so don't get rattled. We ain't going to die. Here, hold this."

Archer held the stick, blowing upon it, while Tom heated an end of the wire, holding the other end in some of the damp straw. As soon as it became red hot he poked it into the place he had selected above him. It took a long time and many heatings to burn a hole an eighth of an inch deep in the thick planking, and their task was not made the pleasanter by the thought that after all it was like taking a shot in the dark. It seemed like an hour, the piece of splintered wood was burned almost away, and what little temper there was in the malleable wire was quite gone from it, when Tom triumphantly pushed it through the hole.

"Strike anything?" Archer asked, in suspense.

"No," said Tom, disappointed. He bent the wire and, as best he could, poked it around outside. "I think I can feel it, though. Missed it by about an inch. There's no use getting discouraged. We'll just have to bore another one."

Long afterward, Archibald Archer often recalled the patience and doggedness which Tom displayed that night.

"As long's the first hole has helped us to find something out, it's worth while, anyway," he said philosophically.

Resolutely he went to work again, like the traditional spider climbing the wall, heating the almost limp wire and by little burnings of a sixteenth of an inch or so at a time he succeeded in making another hole through the heavy planking. But this time the wire encountered a metallic obstruction. Sure enough, Tom could feel the troublesome hasp, but alas, the wire was now too limber to push it up.

"I can just joggle it a little," he said, "but it's too heavy for this wire."

However, by dint of doubling and twisting the wire, he succeeded after many attempts and innumerable straightenings of the wire, in joggling the stubborn hasp free from the padlock eye on which it had barely caught.

"There it goes!" he said with a note of triumph in his usually impassive voice.

Instantly Archer's hands were against the door ready to push it up.

"Wait a minute," whispered Tom; "don't fly off the handle. How do we know who's wandering round? Sh-h! Think I want to run plunk into the Prussian soldier that walked over our heads? Take your time."

In his excitement Archer had forgotten that ominous tread above their prison, and he drew back while Tom raised the door to the merest crack and peered cautiously out. The fresh air afforded them infinite relief.

The night was still and clear, the sky thick with stars. Far away a range of black heights was outlined against the sky, and over there the moon was rising. It seemed to be stealthily creeping up out of that battle-scourged plain in France for a glimpse of

Alsace. It was from beyond those mountains that had come the portentous rumblings which they had heard.

"The blue Alsatian mountains," murmured Tom. "I wish we were across them."

"We'll have to go down and around if we everr get therre," Archer said.

"Sh-h-h!" warned Tom, putting his head out and peering about while Archer held the lid up.

The moonlight, glinting down through the interstices of the trellised vine, made animated shadows in the quiet vineyard, conjuring the wooden supports and knotty masses of vine stalk into lurking human forms. Here some grim figure waited in silence behind an upright, only to dissolve with the changing light. There an ominous helmet seemed to stir amid the thick growth.

The two fugitives, elated at their deliverance, but tremblingly apprehensive, stood hesitating at so radical a move as complete emergence from their hiding place.

"We can't crawl out of herre in daylight, that's surre," whispered Archer. "D'you think maybe she'll come even now - if we waited?"

"It must be long after midnight," Tom answered. "You wait here and hold the door up while I crawl out. Don't move and don't speak. What's that shining over there? See?"

"Nothin' but an old waterring can."

"All right - sh-h-h!"

Cautiously, silently, Tom crept out, peering anxiously in every direction. Stealthily he raised himself. Then suddenly he made a low sound and with a rapidity which startled Archer, dropped to his hands and knees.

"What's the matterr?" Archer whispered. "Come inside - quick!"

But Tom was engrossed with something on the ground.

"What is it?" Archer whispered anxiously. "His footprints?"

"Yop," said Tom, less cautiously. "Come on out. He's standing over there in the field now. Come on out, don't be scared."

Archer did not know what to make of it, but he crept out and looked over to the adjacent field where Tom pointed. A kindly, patient cow, one of those they had seen before, was grazing quietly, partaking of a late lunch in the moonlight.

"Here's her footprint," said Tom simply. "She gave us a good scare, anyway."

"Well - I'll - be -" Archer began.

"Sh-h!" warned Tom. "We don't know yet why Frenchy's sister don't come. But there weren't any soldiers here - that's one sure thing. We had a lot of worry for nothin'. Come on."

## CHAPTER VIII

## THE HOME FIRE NO LONGER BURNS

"That's the first time I was everr scarred by a cow," said Archer, his buoyant spirit fully revived, "but when I hearrd those footsteps overr my head, *go-od night!* It's good you happened to think about looking for footprints, hey?"

"I didn't *happen* to," said Tom. "I always do. Same as you never forget to get a souvenir," he added soberly.

"I'd like to get a sooveneerr from that cow, hey? *You* needn't talk; if it hadn't been for that wire, where'd we be now? Sooveneerrs arre all right. But I admit you've got to have ideas to go with 'em."

"Thanks," said Tom.

"Keep the change," said Archer jubilantly. "Believe me, I don't carre what becomes of me as long as I'm above ground - on terra cotta -"

"We've got to get away from here before daylight, so come on," interrupted Tom.

"Are we going up to the house?"

"What else can we do?"

The explanation of those appalling footfalls by no means explained the failure of Florette to keep her promise, and the fugitives started along the path which led to the house.

They walked very cautiously, Tom scrutinizing the earth-covered planking for any sign of recent passing. The door of the stone kitchen stood open, which surprised them, and they stole quietly inside. A lamp stood upon the table, but there was no sign of human presence.

Tom led the way on tiptoe through the passage where they had passed before, and into the main room where another lamp revealed a ghastly sight. The heavy shutters were closed and barred, just as Florette had closed them when she had brought the boys into the room. Upon the floor lay old Pierre, quite dead, with a cruel wound, as from some blunt instrument, upon his forehead. His whitish gray hair, which had made him look so noble and benignant, was stained with his own blood. Blood lay in a pool about his fine old head, and the old coat which he wore had been torn from him, showing the stump of the arm which he had so long ago given to his beloved France.

Near him lay sprawled upon the floor a soldier in a gray uniform, also dead. A little bullet wound in his temple told the tale. Beside him was a black helmet with heavy brass chin gear. Archer picked it up with trembling hands. Across its front was a motto:

"*Mitt Gott - und Vaterland.*"

The middle of it was obscured by the flaring German coat-of-arms. A pistol lay midway between the two bodies and part of an old engraved motto was still visible on that. Tom could make out the name Napoleon.

"What d'you s'pose happened?" whispered Archer, aghast.

Tom shook his head. "Come on," said he. "Let's look for the others."

Taking the lamp, he led the way silently through the other rooms. On a couch in one of these was laid a soldier's uniform and a loose paper upon the floor showed that it had but lately been unwrapped. There was no sign of Florette or her mother, and Tom felt somewhat relieved at this, for he had feared to find them dead also.

"What d'you think it means?" Archer asked again, as they returned to the room of death.

"I suppose they came for her just like she said," Tom answered in a low tone. "Her father must have shot the soldier, and probably whoever killed the old man took her and her mother away."

He looked down at the white, staring face of old Pierre and thought of how the old soldier had risen from his seat and had stood waiting with his fine military air at the moment of his own arrival at the shadowed and stricken home. He remembered how the old man had waited eagerly for his daughter to translate his and Archer's talk and of his humiliation at the shabby hospitality he must offer them. He took the helmet, a grim-looking thing, from the table where Archer had laid it, and read again, "Mitt Gott -"

It seemed to Tom that this was all wrong - that God must surely be on the side of old Pierre, no matter what had happened.

"Do you know what I think?" he said simply. "I think it was just the way I said - and like she said. They came to get her and maybe they didn't treat her just right, and her father hit one of them. Or maybe he shot him first off. Anyway, I think that soldier suit must be the one Frenchy had to wear, 'cause he told me that the boys in Alsace had to drill even before they got out of school. I guess she was going to bring it to us so one of us could wear it.... We got to feel sorry for her, that's one sure thing."

It was Tom's simple, blunt way of expressing the sympathy which surged up in his heart.

"I liked her; she treated us fine," said Archer.

For a few seconds Tom did not answer; then he said in his old stolid way, "I don't know where they took her or what they'll make her do, but anybody could see she didn't have any muscle. Whenever I think of her I'll fight harder, that's one sure thing."

For a few moments he could hardly command himself as he contemplated this tragic end of the broken home. Florette, whom he had seen but yesterday, had been taken away - away from her home, probably from her beloved Alsace, to enforced labor for the Teuton tyrant. He recalled her slender form as she hurried through the darkness ahead of them, her gentle apology for their poor reception, her wistful memories of her brother as she showed them their hiding-place, her touching grief and apprehension as she stood talking with him under the trellis....

And now she was gone and awful thoughts of her peril and suffering welled up in Tom's mind.

He looked at the stark figure and white, staring face of old Pierre and thought of the impetuous embrace the old man had given him. He thought of his friend, Frenchy. And the mother - where was she? Good people, kind people; trying in the menacing shadow of the detestable Teuton beast to keep their flickering home fire burning. And this was the end of it.

Most of all, he thought of Florette and her wistful, fearful look haunted him. "*Maybe for ze great Krupps*" - the phrase lingered in his mind and he stood there appalled at the realization of this awful, unexplained thing which had happened.

Then Tom Slade did something which his scout training had taught him to do, while Archer, tremulous and unstrung, stood awkwardly by, watching. He knelt down over the lifeless form of the old man and straightened the prostrate figure so that it lay becomingly and decently upon the hard floor. He bent the one arm and laid it across the breast in the usual posture of dignity and peace. He took the threadbare covering from the old melodeon and placed it over the face. So that the last service for old Pierre Leteur was performed by an American boy; and at least the ashes of the home fire were left in order by a scout from far across the seas.

"It's part of first aid," explained Tom quietly, as he rose; "I learned how at Temple Camp."

Archer said nothing.

"When a scout from Maryland died up there, I saw how they did it."

"You got to thank the scouts for a lot," said Archer; "forr trackin' an' trailin' -"

"'Tain't on account of them," said Tom, his voice breaking a little, "it's on account of her -"

And he kneeled again to arrange the corner of the cloth more neatly over the wrinkled, wounded face....

# CHAPTER IX

## FLIGHT

"Anyway, we've got to get away from here quick," said Tom, pulling himself together; "never mind about clothes or anything. One thing sure, they'll be back here soon. See if he has a watch," he added, indicating the dead soldier.

"No, but he's got a little compass around his neck; shall I take it?"

"Sure, we got a right to capture anything from the enemy."

"He's got some papers, too."

"All right, take 'em. Come on out through the kitchen way - hurry up. Don't make any noise. You look for some food - I'll be with you right away."

Tom crept cautiously out to the road and, kneeling, placed his ear to the ground. There was no sound, and he hurried back to the stone kitchen where Archer was stuffing his pockets with such dry edibles as he could gather.

"All right, come on," he whispered hurriedly. "What have you got?"

"Some hard bread and a couple of salt fish -"

"Give me one of those," Tom interrupted: "and hand me that tablecloth. Come on. Got some matches?"

"Yes, and a candle, too."

"Good. Don't strike a light. You go ahead, along the plank walk."

Leaving the scene of the tragedy, they hurried along the board walk under the trellis, Tom dragging the tablecloth so that it swept both of the narrow planks and obliterated any suggestion of footprints. When they had gone about fifty yards he stooped and flung the salt fish from him so that it barely skimmed the earth and rested at some distance from the path.

"If they should have any dogs with 'em, that'll take 'em off the trail," he said.

"I'm sorry I didn't get you a souveneerr too," said Archer, as they hurried along.

This was the first intimation Tom had that Archer regarded the little compass merely as a souvenir.

"You can give me those papers you took," he said, half in joke.

"It's only an envelope," Archer said. "Have you got your button all right?"

"Sure."

When they reached the wine vat, Tom threw the old tablecloth into it, and pulled the vine more carefully so as to conceal the door. They were tempted to rest here, but realized that if they spent the balance of the night in their former refuge it would mean another long day in the dank hole.

The vineyard ended a few yards from the wine vat and beyond was an area of open lowlands across which the boys could see a range of low wooded hills.

"We've got about four hours till daylight," said Tom; "let's make for those woods."

"That's east," said Archer. "*We* want to go south."

"We want to see where we're going before we go anywhere," Tom answered. "If we can get into the woods on those hills, we can climb a tree tomorrow and see where we're at. What I want is a bird's-eye squint to start off with, 'cause we can't ask questions of anybody."

"No, and believe me, we don't want to run into any cities," said Archer. "We got through one night anyway, hey?"

Notwithstanding that they were without shelter, and facing the innumerable perils of a hostile country about which they knew nothing, they still found action preferable to inaction and their spirits rose as they journeyed on with the star-studded sky overhead.

They found the meadows low and marshy, which gratified Tom who was always fearful of leaving footprints. The hills beyond were low and thickly wooded, the face of the nearest being broken by slides and forming almost a precipice surmounted by a jumble of rocks and underbrush. The country seemed wild and isolated enough.

"I suppose it's the beginning of the Alps, maybe," Tom panted as they scrambled up.

"There's nobody up here, that's surre," Archer answered.

"We'll just lie low till daylight and see if we can get a squint at the country. Then tomorrow night we'll hike it south. If we go straight south we've *got* to come to Switzerland."

"It's lucky we've got the compass," said Archer.

"Maybe this is a ridge we're on," Tom said. "If it is, we're in luck. We may be able to go thirty or forty miles along it. One thing sure, it'll be more hilly the farther south we get 'cause we'll be getting into the beginning of the Alps. There ought to be water up here."

"I wish there were some apples," said Archer.

"You're always thinking about apples and souvenirs. Let's crawl in under here."

They had scrambled to the top of the precipitous ascent and found themselves upon the broken edge of the forest amid a black chaos of piled up rock and underbrush. Evidently, the land here was giving way, little by little, for here and there they could see a tree canting tipsily over the edge, its network of half-exposed roots making a last gallant stand against the erosive process and helping to hold the weight of the great boulders which ere long would crash down into the marshy lowlands.

They crept into a sort of leafy cave formed by a fallen tree and stretched their weary bodies and relaxed their tense nerves after what had seemed a nightmare.

"As long as we're going to join the army," said Tom, "we might as well make a rule now. We won't both sleep at the same time till we're out of Germany. We got to live up to that rule no matter how tired we get."

"I'm game," said Archer. "You go to sleep now and when I get good and sleepy I'll wake you up."

"In about two hours," said Tom. "Then you can sleep till it's light. Then we'll see if it's safe to stay here. Keep looking in that direction - the way we came. And if you see any lights, wake me up."

Archer did not obey these directions at all, for he sat with his hands clasped over his knees, gazing down across the dark marshland below. Two hours, three hours, four hours, he sat there and scarcely stirred. And as the time dragged on and there were no lights and no sounds he took fresh courage and hope. He was beginning to realize the value of the stolid determination, the resourcefulness, the keen eye and stealthy foot and clear brain of the comrade who lay sleeping at his side. He had wanted to tell Tom Slade what he thought of him and how he trusted him, but he did not know how. So he just sat there, hour in and hour out, and let the weary pathfinder of Temple Camp sleep until he awoke of his own accord.

"All right," said Archer then, blinking. "Nothing happened."

# CHAPTER X

## THE SOLDIER'S PAPERS

All that day they stayed in their leafy refuge. They could look down across the marshy meadows they had crossed to the trellised vineyard of the Leteurs, looking orderly and symmetrical in the distance like a two-storied field, and beyond that the massive gables of the gray, forsaken house.

They could see the whole neighboring country in panorama. Other houses were discernible at infrequent intervals along the road which wound southward through the lowland between the hills where the boys were and the Vosges Mountains (the "Blue Alsatian Mountains") to the west. Through the long, daylight hours Tom studied the country carefully. Now, as never before (for he knew how much depended on it), he watched for every scrap of knowledge which might afford any inference or deduction to help them in their flight.

"You can see how it is," he told Archer, as they watched the little compass needle, waiting for it to settle. "This is a ridge and it runs north and south. I kind of think it's the west side of the valley of a river, like Daggett's Hills are to Perch River up your way."

"I'd like to be therre now," said Archer.

"I'd rather be in France," Tom answered.

"Of course it'll fizzle out in places and we'll come to villages, but there's enough woods ahead of us for us to go twenty miles tonight. That's the way it seems to me, anyway."

Once Tom ventured out on hands and knees into the woods in quest of water, and returned with the good news that he had had a refreshing drink from a brook to which he directed Archer.

"Do you know what this is?" he said, emptying an armful of weeds on the ground. "It's chicory. If I dared to build a fire I could make you a good imitation of coffee with that. But we can eat the roots, anyway. Now I remember it used to be in the geography in school about so much chicory growing in the Alps -"

"Oh, Ebeneezerr!" shouted Archer, much to Tom's alarm. "I'm glad you said that 'cause it reminds me about the mussels."

"The *what?*"

"'The mountain streams abound with the pearrl-bearing mussels which are a staple article of diet with the Alpine natives,'" quoted Archer in declamatory style. "I had to write that two hundred and fifty times frr whittlin' a hole in the desk -"

"I s'pose you were after a souvenir," said Tom dryly.

"Firrst I wrote it once 'n' then I put two hundred and forty-nine ditto marrks. *Ebenezerr!* Wasn't the teacherr mad! I had to write it two hundred and fifty times frr vandalism and two hundred and fifty morre frr insolence."

"Served you right," said Tom.

"Oh, I guess you weren't such an angel in school either!" said Archer. "I'll never forget about those pearrl-bearing mussels as long as I live - you can bet!"

Tom separated the chicory roots from the stalks and Archer went to wash them in the stream. In a little while he returned with a triumphant smile all over his round, freckled face and half a dozen mussels in his cupped hands.

"*Now* what have you got to say, huh? It's good I whittled that desk and was insolent - you can bet!"

Tom's practical mind did not quite appreciate this line of reasoning, but he was glad enough to see the mussels, the very look of which was cool and refreshing.

"I always said I had no use for geographies except to put mustaches and things on the North Pole explorers and high hats on Columbus and Henry Hudson, but, believe *me*, I'm glad I remembered about those pearrl-bearing mussels - hey, Slady? I hope the Alpine natives don't take it into their heads to come up herre afterr any of 'em just now. I just rooted around in the mud and got 'em. Look at my hand, will you?"

They made a sumptuous repast of wet, crisp chicory roots and "pearrl-bearing mussels" as Archer insisted upon calling them, although they found no pearls. The meal was refreshing and not half bad. There was a pleasant air of stealth and cosiness about the whole thing, lying there in their leafy refuge in the edge of the woods with the Alsatian country stretched below them. Perhaps it was the mussels out of the geography (to quote Archer's own phrase) as well as the sense of security which came as the uneventful hours passed, but as the twilight gathered they enjoyed a feeling of safety, and their hope ran high. They had found, as the scout usually finds, that Nature was their friend, never withholding her bounty from him who seeks and uses his resourcefulness and brains.

All through the long afternoon they could distinguish heavy army wagons with dark spots on their canvas sides (the flaring, arrogant German crest which allied soldiers had grown to despise) moving northward along the distant road. They looked almost like toy wagons. Sometimes, when the breeze favored, they could hear the rattle of wheels and occasionally a human voice was faintly audible. And all the while from those towering heights beyond came the spent, muffled booming.

"I'd like to know just what's going on over there," Tom said as he gazed at the blue heights. "Maybe those wagons down there on the road have something to do with it. If there's a big battle going on they may be bringing back wounded and prisoners. - Some of our own fellers might be in 'em."

They tried to determine about where, along that far-flung line, the sounds arose, but they could only guess at it.

"All I know is what I hearrd 'em say in the prison camp," said Archer; "that our fellers are just the otherr side of the mountains."

"That would be Nancy," said Tom thoughtfully.

"That Loquet feller that got capturred in a raid," Archer said, "told me the Americans were all around therre, just the otherr side of the mountains - in a lot of differrent villages: When they get through training they send 'em ahead to the trenches. Some of 'em have been in raids already, he said."

"You have to run like everything in a raid," said Tom. "I'd like to be in one, wouldn't you?"

"Depends on which way I was running. - Let's have a look at these paperrs before it gets too darrk, hey?" he added, hauling from his pocket the papers which he had taken from the dead Boche. "I neverr thought about 'em till just now?"

"I thought about it," said Tom, who indeed seldom forgot anything, "but I didn't say anything about it 'cause it kind of makes me think about what happened - I mean how they took her away," he added, in his dull way.

For a minute they sat silently gazing down at the vineyard

which was now touched with the first crimson rays of sunset.

"You can just see the chimney," Tom said; "see, just left of that big tree. - I hope I don't see Frenchy any more now 'cause I wouldn't like to have to tell him -"

"We don't know what happened," said Archer. "Maybe therre werren't any otherr soldierrs; she may have escaped - and her motherr, too."

"It's more likely there *were* others, though," said Tom. "I keep thinking all the time how scared she was and it kind of -"

"Let's look at the papers," said Archer.

The German soldier must have been a typical Boche, for he carried with him the customary baggage of written and statistical matter with which these warriors sally forth to battle.

"He must o' been a walking correspondence school," said Archer, unfolding the contents of the parchment envelope. "Herre's a list - all in German. Herre's some poetry - or I s'pose it's poetry, 'cause it's printed all in and out."

"Maybe it's a hymn of hate," said Tom.

"Herre's a map, and herre's a letter. All in Gerrman - even the map. Anyway, I can't understand it."

"Looks like a scout astronomy chart," said Tom. "It's all dots like the big dipper."

"Do you s'pose it means they're going to conquer the sky and all the starrs and everything?" Archer asked. "Here's a letter, it's dated about two weeks ago - I can make out the numbers all right."

The letter was in German, of course, and Archer, who during his long incarceration in the prison camp had picked up a few scraps of the language, fell to trying to decipher it. The only reward he had for his pains was a familiar word which he was able to distinguish here and there and which greatly increased their desire to know the full purport of the letter.

"Herre's President Wilson's name. - See!" said Archer excitedly. "And herre's *America* -"

"Yes, and there it is again," said Tom. "That must be *Yankees*, see? Something or other Yankees. It's about a mile long."

"Jim-min-nitty!" said Archer, staring at the word (presumably a disparaging adjective) which preceded the word *Yankees*. "It's got one - two - three - wait a minute - it's got thirty-seven letters to it. *Go-o-od night!*"

"And that must be Arracourt," said Tom. "I heard about that place - it ain't so far from Nancy. Gee, I wish we could read that letter!"

"I'd like to know what kind of a Yankee a b-l-o-e -"

But Archer gave it up in despair.

# CHAPTER XI

## THE SCOUT THROUGH ALSACE

As soon as it was dark they started southward, following the ridge. Their way took them up hill and down dale, through rugged uplands where they had to travel five miles to advance three, picking their way over the trackless, rocky heights which formed the first foothills of the mighty Alps.

"S'pose we should meet some one?" Archer suggested, as he followed Tom's lead over the rocky ledges.

"Not up here," said Tom. "You can see lights way off south and maybe we'll have to pass through some villages tomorrow night, but not tonight. We'll only do about twelve miles tonight if it keeps up like this."

"S'pose somebody should see us - when we'rre going through a village? We'll tell him we'rre herre to back the Kaiser, hey?"

"S'pose he's a Frenchman that belongs in Alsace," Tom queried.

"Then we'll add on *out o' France*. We'll say - look out for that rock! - We'll just say we'rre herre to back the Kaiser, and if he looks sourr we'll say; *out o' France. Back the Kaiser out o' France.* We win either way, see? A fellerr in prison told me General Perrshing wants a lot of men with glass eyes - to peel onions. Look out you don't trip on that root! Herre's anotherr.

If you'rre under sixteen what part of the arrmy do they put you in? The infantry, of course. Herre's -"

"Never mind," laughed Tom. "Look where you're stepping."

"What I'm worrying about now," said Archer, his spirits mounting as they made their way southward, "is how we're going to cross the frontierr when we get to it. They've got a big tangled fence of barrbed wirre all along, even across the mountains, to where the battleline cuts in. And it's got a good juicy electric current running through it all the time. If you just touch it - good night!"

"I got an idea," said Tom simply.

"If I could get a piece of that electrified wirre for a souveneerr," mused Archer, "I'd -"

"You'll have a broken head for a souvenir in a minute," said Tom, "if you don't watch where you're going."

"Gee, you've got eyes in your feet," said Archer admiringly.

"Whenever you see a fallen tree," said Tom, "look out for holes. It means the earth is thin and weak all around and couldn't hold the roots."

"It ought to drink buttermilk, hey?" said Archer flippantly, "if it's thin and pale."

"I said thin and weak," said Tom. "Do you ever get tired talking?"

"Sure - same as a phonograph record does."

So they plodded on, encircling areas of towering rock or surmounting them when they were not too high, and always working southward. Tom, who was not unaccustomed to woods and mountains, thought he had never before traversed such a chaotic wilderness. He would have given a good deal for a watch and for some means of knowing how much actual distance they were covering. It was slow, tiresome work.

Every little while he would check their course by the little compass, to see which he often had to light one of their few precious matches.

"One thing surre, we won't meet anybody up herre," said Archer, as he scrambled along. "See those little lights over to the east?"

"Don't worry," said Tom, "that's twenty miles away. We're all right up here. There were some lights further down too and one over that way but I can't see them now. I guess it's after midnight. Sh-h-h. Listen!"

They stood stark still, Archer gripping Tom's arm.

"It's water trickling," said Tom dully.

"Gee, you had the life scared out of me!" breathed Archer.

A little farther on they came to an abrupt, rocky declivity which crossed their course and in the bottom of which was a swift running stream.

"It's running east," said Tom, listening intently. "I can tell by the ripples."

"Yes, you can!" said Archer contemptuously.

"Sure I can," Tom answered. He held his hand first to his right ear, then to his left. "The long, washy sound comes first when you close your left ear, so I know the water's flowing that way. It's easy," he added.

They kept along the precipitous brink, searching for a place to descend and at last scrambled down and into the shallow stream.

"Didn't I tell you so?" said Tom, laying a twig in the water and watching it as best he could in the dim light. "What's on the east of Alsace, anyway?"

"Another parrt of Gerrmany - Baden," Archer answered.

"I was wondering where this stream goes," Tom said; "let's walk along in it a little way and go up at a different place. They can't track you in the water."

"I bet *you* could," said Archer admiringly.

"Let's have a drink and give me a couple of those chicory roots, and I'll show you something," Tom said.

From each chicory root he cut a plug such as one cuts to test the flavor of a watermelon. Then he soaked the roots in the stream. "The inside's softer than the outside," he said, "and it holds the water." After a few moments he replaced the plugs. "Even tomorrow," he added, "they'll be fresh and cool and they'll quench your thirst. Carrots are best but we haven't got any carrots."

About fifty yards down stream they turned out of it and scrambled up a less abrupt hillside and into an area of more or less orderly forest.

"Maybe it's the Black Forest," said Archer; "anyway it's black enough. Look around and you'll probably see some toys - jumping-jacks and things. 'Most all the toys like that arre made in the Black Forest."

"Not here," said Tom; "we won't find anybody in here."

They were indeed entering the less densely wooded region which formed the extreme northern reaches of that mountainous wilderness famed in song and story as the Black Forest.

Even here, where it fizzled out on the eastern edge of Alsace, the world-renowned fragrance of its dark and stately fir trees was wafted to them out of the wild and solemn recesses they were approaching.

"I wish I had a map," said Tom.

"We ought to be thankful we've got the compass. If this *is* the Black Forest, you can bet I'm going to get a sooveneer. Gee, isn't it dark! It smells good though, believe *me*."

They passed on now over land comparatively level, the soft, fragrant needles yielding under their feet, the tall cone-like trees diffusing their resiny, pungent odor. It seemed as if the war must be millions of miles away. The silence was deathlike and the occasional crunching of a cone under their feet startled them as they groped their way in the heavy darkness.

"That looks like an oak ahead," said Archer. "You can see the branches sticking out -"

"Sh-h-h," said Tom, grasping his arm suddenly and speaking in a tense whisper. "Look - right under it - don't move -"

Archer looked intently and under the low spreading branches he saw a human form with something shiny upon its head. As the two boys paused, awestruck and shaking, it moved ever so slightly.

The fugitives stood rooted to the ground, breathing in quick, short gasps, their hearts pounding in their breasts.

"He didn't see us," whispered Tom, in the faintest whisper. "Wait till there's a breeze and get behind a tree."

When presently the breeze rustled in the tress the two moved cautiously behind two trees.

And the silent figure moved also....

# CHAPTER XII

## THE DANCE WITH DEATH

The boys were thoroughly frightened, but they stood absolutely motionless and silent and Tom, at least, retained his presence of mind. They were not close enough together to communicate with each other, nor could they more than distinguish each other's forms pressed against the dark tree trunks.

But the figure, being comparatively in the open, was discernible and Tom, by concentrating his eyes upon it, satisfied himself beyond a doubt that it was a human form - that of a German soldier, he felt sure.

Thanks to his stealth and dexterity, they were apparently undiscovered. He tried to distinguish the bright spot on the cap or helmet, but it was not visible now, and he thought the man must have turned about.

In his alarm it seemed to him that his breathing must be audible miles away. His heart seemed in his throat and likely to choke him with every fresh breath. But he did not stir. Then another little breeze stirred the trees, sounding clear and solemn in the stillness and Tom moved ever so slightly in unison with it, hoping by changing his angle of vision to catch a better glimpse. He could see the bright spot now, the grim figure standing directly facing him in ghostly silence.

No one moved. And there was no sound save the half audible rustle of some tiny creature of the night as it hurried over the cushiony ground.

What did it mean? Who was it, standing there? Some grim Prussian sentinel? Had they, in this remote wilderness, stumbled upon some obscure pass which the all-seeing eye of German militarism had not forgotten? Was there, after all, any hope of escape from these demons of efficiency?

Archer, his chest literally aching from his throbbing breaths, crowded close behind his tree trunk in terror, startled by every fresh stir of the fragrant breeze. It seemed to him, as he looked, that the figure danced a trifle, but doubtless that was only his tense nerves and blinking eyes playing havoc with his imagination.

There was another rustling in the trees, caused by the freshening night breeze which Tom thought smelt of rain. And again the silent figure veered around with a kind of mechanical precision, the very perfection of clock-work German discipline, as if to give each point of the compass its allotted moment of attention.

Tom strained his eyes, trying to discover whether that lonely sentinel were standing in a path or where two paths crossed or where some favored view might be had of something far off in the country below. But he could make out nothing.

Suddenly he noticed something large and black among the trees. Its outline was barely discernible against the less solid blackness of the night, and it was obscured by the dark tree branches. But as he looked he thought he could see that it terminated in a little dome, like the police telephone booths on the street corners away home in Bridgeboro. A tiny guard-house, possibly, or shelter for the solitary sentinel. Perhaps, he thought, this was, after all, a strategic spot which they had unconsciously stumbled into; a secret path to the frontier, maybe.

He remembered now the talk he had heard in the prison camp, of Germany's building roads through obscure places in the direction of the Swiss border for the violation of Swiss neutrality if that should be thought necessary. These roads were shrouded in mystery, but he had heard about them and the thought occurred to him that perhaps these poor Alsatian people - women and children - were being taken to work on these avenues of betrayal and dishonor.

But try as he would, he could discern no suggestion of path, nor any other sign of landmark which might explain the presence of this remote station in the desolate uplands of Alsace. He believed that if they had taken five steps more they would have been discovered and challenged. How to withdraw out of the very jaws of this peril was now the question. He feared that Archer might make an incautious move and end all hope of escape.

Tom watched the solitary figure through the heavy darkness. And he marvelled, as he had marvelled before, at the machine-like perfection of these minions of the Iron Hand. Even in the face of their awful danger and amid the solemnity of the black night, the odd thought came to him that this stiff form turning about like a faithful and tireless weathercock to peer into the darkness roundabout, might be indeed a huge carved toy fresh from the quaint handworkers of the Black Forest.

As he gazed he was sure that this lonely watcher danced a step or two. No laughter or sign of merriment accompanied the grim jig, but he was sure that the solitary German tripped, ever so lightly, with a kind of stiff grace. Then the freshening breeze blew Tom's rebellious hair down over his eyes, and as he brushed it aside he saw the German indeed dancing - there was no doubt of it.

Suddenly a cold shudder ran through him and he stepped out from his concealment as he realized that this uncanny figure was not standing but *hanging* just clear of the ground.

# CHAPTER XIII

## THE PRIZE SAUSAGE

"Come on out, Archy," said Tom with a recklessness which struck terror to poor Archer's very soul. "He won't hurt you - he's dead."

"D-e-a-d!" ejaculated Archer.

"Sure - he's hanging there."

"And all the time I wanted to sneeze," said Archer, laughing in his reaction from fear. "Ebe-nee-zerr, but I had a good scarre!"

Going over to the tree, they saw the ghastly truth. A man wearing a garment something like a Russian blouse, but of the field-gray military shade of the Germans (as well as the boys could make out by the aid of a lighted match) was hanging by his garment which had caught in a low spreading branch of the tree. His feet were just clear of the ground and as the breeze blew he swayed this way and that, the gathering strain upon his garment behind the neck throwing his limp head forward and giving his shoulders a hunched appearance, quite in the manner of the clog dancer. The German emblem was blazoned upon his blouse and superimposed in shining metal upon the front of his fatigue cap. Even as they paused before him he seemed to bow perfunctorily as if bidding them a ghastly welcome.

Percy Keese Fitzhugh

Tom's scout instinct impelled him instantly to fall upon the ground in search of enlightening footprints, but there were none and this puzzled him greatly. He felt sure that the man had not been strangled, but had been killed by impact with some heavier branch higher up in the tree; but he must have made footprints before he climbed the tree, and -

Suddenly he jumped to his feet, remembering what he had thought to be a guardhouse. It lay a hundred or more feet beyond the dangling body and as they neared it it lost its sentinel-station aspect altogether.

"Well - what - do you - know about that?" said Archer.

"It's an observation balloon, I'll bet," said Tom. "A Boche sausage! Look for another man before you do anything else - there's always two. If he's around anywhere we might get into trouble yet."

It was a wise thought and characteristic of Tom, but the other man was quite beyond human aid. He lay, mangled out of all semblance to a human being, amid the tangled wreckage of the car.

The fat cigar-shaped envelope of the balloon stood almost upright, and though it looked not the least like a police telephone station now, it was easy to see how, from a distance in the dim light, it might have suggested a little round domed building.

"How do you s'pose it happened?" Archer asked.

"I don't know," said Tom. "It's an observation balloon, that's sure. Maybe it was on its way back from the lines to somewhere or other. Hurry up, let's see what there is; it'll be daylight in two or three hours and we don't want to be hanging around here. They might send a rescue party or something like that, if they know about it."

"Morre likely they don't," said Archer.

"I guess it only happened tonight," said Tom, "or more gas would have leaked out. Let's hunt for the eats and things."

The wreckage of the car proved a veritable treasure-house. There was a flashlight and a telescopic field glass, both of which Tom snatched up with an eagerness which could not have been greater if they had been made of solid gold. In the smashed locker were two good-sized tins of biscuit, a bottle of wine and several small tins of meat. Tom emptied out the wine and filled the bottle with water out of the five-gallon tank, from which they also refreshed their parched throats. The food they "commandeered" to the full capacity of their ragged pockets.

"And look at this," said Archer, hauling out a blouse such as the hanging German wore; "what d'ye say if I wearr it, hey? And the cap, too? I'll look like an observation ballooner, or whatever you call 'em."

"Good idea," said Tom, "and look!"

"A souveneerr?" cried Archer.

"The best *you* ever saw," Tom answered, rooting in the engine tool chest by the aid of the flashlight and hauling out a pair of rubber gloves.

"What good are those?" said Archer, somewhat scornfully.

"*What good!* They're a passport into Switzerland."

"Do you have to wear rubber gloves in Switzerland?" Archer asked innocently, as he ravenously munched a biscuit.

"No, but you have to wear 'em when you're handling electrified wire," said Tom in his stolid way.

"G-o-o-d *night*! We fell in soft, didn't we!"

Indeed, for a couple of hapless, ragged wanderers, subsisting wholly by their wits, they had "fallen in soft." It seemed that the very things needed by two fugitives in a hostile country were the very things needed in an observation balloon. One unpleasant task Tom had to perform, and that was to remove the blouse from the hanging German and don it himself, which he did, not without some shuddering hesitation.

"It's the only thing," he said, "that would make anybody think somebody's been here, and that's just what we've got to look out for. The other things won't be missed, but if anybody should come here and see him hanging there without his coat they'd wonder where it was."

However, this was a remote danger, since probably no one knew of the disaster.

Tom's chief difficulty was in restricting that indefatigable souvenir hunter, Archer, from loading himself down with every conceivable kind of useless but interesting paraphernalia.

"You're just like a tenderfoot when he starts out camping," said Tom. "He takes fancy cushions and a lot of stuff; he'd take a brass bed and a rolltop desk and a couple of pianos if you'd let him," he added, with rather more humor than he usually showed. "All we're going to take is the biscuits and two cans of meat and the flashlight and the field glass and the bottle, and, let's see -"

"I don't have to leave this dandy ivory cigar-holderr, do I?" Archer interrupted. "We could use it for -"

"Yes, you do, and we're going to leave that cartridge belt, too, so chuck it," ordered Tom. "If anybody *should* come up here we don't want 'em to think somebody else was here before 'em. All we're going to take is just what I said - some of the eats, and the flashlight and the field glass and the bottle and the rubber gloves and the pliers and - that's all."

"Not even this dial-faced thing?" pleaded Archer.

"That's a gas gauge or something," said Tom. "Come on now, let's get away from here."

Archer pointed the flashlight and cast a lingering farewell gaze upon a large megaphone. For a brief moment he had wild thoughts of trying to persuade Tom that this would prove a blessing as a hat, shedding the pelting Alsatian rains like a church steeple. But he did not quite dare.

Percy Keese Fitzhugh

eastern edge of Alsace where the Rhine, flowing in a northeasterly direction, separates the "lost province" from the Duchy of Baden. To the south, on the Baden side, the mighty hills rolled away in crowding confusion as far as they could see, and these they knew held that dim, romantic wilderness, the Black Forest, the outskirts of which they had entered.

Directly below the hill on which they rested was a tiny hamlet nestling in the shadow of the steep ascent, and when Tom climbed a tree for a better view he could see to the southwest close by the river a surging metropolis with countless chimneys sending their black smoke up into the gray early morning sky.

"I bet it's Berrlin," shouted Archer. "Gee, we'll be the firrst to get therre, hey? It might be Berrlin, hey?" he added with less buoyancy, seeing Tom's dry smile.

"It might be New York or Philadelphia," said Tom, "only it ain't. I guess it must be Strassbourg. I heard that was the biggest place in Alsace."

They looked at it through their field glass and decided that it was about twenty miles distant. More to the purpose was the little hamlet scarce half a mile below them, for their provisions were gone and as Tom scanned the country with the glass he could see no streams to the southward converging toward the river. He feared to have to go another twenty-four hours, perhaps, without food and water.

"We got to decide another thing before we go any farther, too," he said. "If we're going to hike into those mountains we've got to cross the river and we'll be outside of Alsace. We won't meet any French people and Frenchy's button won't do us any good over there. But if we stay on this side we've got to go through open country. I don't know which is better."

They were indeed at a point where they must choose between the doubtful hospitality of Alsace and the safe enveloping welcome of the mountain fastnesses. Like the true scout he was, Tom inclined to the latter.

"Do you notice," he said, looking down through the glass, "that house that looks as if it was whitewashed? It's far away from the others."

Archer took the glass and looking down saw a little white house with a heavy roof of thatch. A tipsy, ramshackle fence surrounded it and in the enclosure several sheep were grazing. The whole poor farm, if such it was, was at the end of a long rustic overgrown lane and quite a distance from the cluster of houses which constituted the hamlet. By scrambling down the rugged hillside one could reach this house without entering the hamlet at all.

"If I dared, I'd make the break," said Tom.

"Suppose they should be Gerrmans living therre?" Archer suggested. "I wouldn't risk it. Can't you see therre's a German flag on a flagpole?"

"That's just it," said Tom. "If I knew they were French people I could show them Frenchy's button. If I was sure this uniform, or whatever you call it, was all right, I'd take a chance."

"It's all right at a distance, anyway," Archer encouraged; "as long as nobody can see yourr face or speak to you."

It was a pretty risky business and both realized it. After three days of successful flight to run into the very jaws of recapture by an ill-considered move was not at all to Tom's liking, yet he felt sure that it would be equally risky to penetrate into that dark wilderness which stretched away toward the Swiss border without first ascertaining something of its extent and character, and what the prospect was of getting through it unseen. Moreover, they were hungry.

Yet it was twilight and the distant river had become a dark

ribbon and the outlines of the poor houses below them blurred and indistinct in the gathering darkness before Tom could bring himself to re-enter the haunts of men.

"You stay here," he said, "and I'll go down and pike around. There's one thing, that house is very old and people don't move around here like they do in America. So if I see anything that makes me think the house is French then probably the people are French too."

It was a sensible thought, more dependable indeed than Tom imagined, for in poor Alsace and Lorraine, of all places, people who loved their homes enough to remain in them under foreign despotism would probably continue living in them generation after generation. There is no moving day in Europe.

# CHAPTER XV

## HE WHO HAS EYES TO SEE

It was quite dark when Tom scrambled down and, with his heart beating rapidly, stole cautiously across the hubbly ground toward the dilapidated brush fence which enclosed the place. The disturbing thought occurred to him that where there were sheep there was likely to be a dog, but he would not turn back.

He realized that he was gambling with those hard-won days of freedom, that any minute he might be discovered and seized. But the courage which his training as a scout had given him did not forsake him, and he crossed the fence and stealthily approached the house, which was hardly more than a whitewashed cabin with two small windows, one door and a disheveled roof, entirely too big for it as it seemed to Tom. The odd conceit occurred to him that it ought to be brushed and combed like a shocky head of hair. Within there was a dim light, and protecting each window was a rough board shutter, hinged at the top and held open at an angle by a stick.

He crept cautiously up and examined these shutters with minutest care. He even felt of one of them and found it to be old and rotten. Then he felt to see if his precious button was safe in his pocket.

Evidently the dilapidated shutter suggested something to him, for he glanced about as if looking for something else, and seemed encouraged. Now he stole a quick look this way or that

Percy Keese Fitzhugh

to anticipate the approach of any one, and then looked carefully about again.

At last his eyes lit upon the flagpole which was projected diagonally from the house, with the flag, which he knew must be the German flag, depending from it. The distant sight of this flag had quite discouraged Archer's hopes, but Tom knew that the compulsory display of the Teuton colors was no indication of the sentiment of the people.

He was more interested in the rough, home-made flagpole which he ventured to bend a little so as to bring its end within reach. This he examined with a care entirely disproportionate to the importance of the crude, whittled handiwork. He pushed the drooping flag aside rather impatiently as it fell over his face, and felt of the end of the pole and scrutinized it as best he could in the darkness.

It was roughly carved and intended to be ornamental, swelling into a kind of curved ridge surmounted by a dull, dome-like point. He felt it all over, then cautiously bending the pole down within reach of his mouth, he bit into the wood and deposited the two or three loose splinters in his pocket.

Then he hurried back up the hill to rejoin Archer.

"Let me have the flashlight," he said with rather more excitement than he often showed. And he would say no more till he had examined the little splinter of wood in its glare.

"It's all right," he said; "we're safe in going there. See this? It's a splinter from the flagpole -"

"A souveneerr!" Archer interrupted.

"There you go again," said Tom. "Who's talking about souvenirs? See how white and fresh the wood is - look. That's off the end of the pole where it's carved into kind of a fancy topknot. And it was whittled inside of a year."

"*I* could whittle it inside of an hour," said Archer.

"I mean it was whittled not longer than a year ago, 'cause even the weather hasn't got into it yet. And it's whittled like a fleur-de-lis - kind of," Tom added triumphantly.

"Why didn't you bring the whole of it?"

"When they were building the shacks at Temple Camp," said Tom, "there was a carpenter who was a Frenchman. I was good friends with him and he told me a lot of stuff. He always had some wine in his dinner pail. He showed me how French carpenters nail shingles. Instead of keeping the nails in their mouths like other carpenters do, they keep them up their sleeves and they can drop them down into their hands one by one as fast as they need them. They hit 'em four times instead of two - do you know why?"

"To drive 'em in," suggested Archer.

"'Cause in France they don't have cedar shingles, like we do; they have shingles made out of hard wood. And they get so used to hitting the nail four raps that they can't stop it - that's what he said."

"Here's another one," said Archer. "You can't drive a nail with a sponge - no matter how you soak it."

"He told me some other things, too," said Tom, ignoring Archer's flippancy. "He used to talk to me while he was eating his lunch. The way he got started telling me about the different way they do things in Europe was when he put the shutters on the big shack. He put the hinges at the top 'cause that's always the way they do in France. He said in Italy they put 'em on the left side. In America they put them on the right side - except when they have two.

"So when I saw the shutters on that old house I happened to notice that the hinges were at the top and that made me think

Percy Keese Fitzhugh

it was probably a Frenchman's home."

"Maybe it isn't now even if it was when the shutterrs werre made," said Archer skeptically.

"Then I happened to remember something else that man told me. Maybe you think the fleur-de-lis is only a fancy kind of an emblem, but it ain't. He told me the old monks that used to carve things - no matter what they carved you could always find a cross, or something like a cross in it. 'Cause they *think* that way, see? The same as sailors always tattoo fishes and ships and things on their arms. He said some places in the Black Forest the toymakers are French peasants and you can always tell if a fancy thing is carved by them on account of the shape of the fleur-de-lis. It ain't that they do it on purpose," he added; "it's because it's in their heads, like. They don't always make regular fleur-de-lis, but they make that kind of curves. He told me a lot about Napoleon, too," he added irrelevantly.

"So when I happened to think about that, I looked around to see if I could find anything to prove it, kind of. It don't make any difference if the German flag *is* on that pole; they've *got* to do that. When I saw the topknot was carved kind of like a fleur-de-lis I knew French people must have made it. And it was only carved lately, too," he added simply, "'cause the wood is fresh."

"Gee whillicums, but you're a peach, Slady!" said Archer ecstatically. "Shall we take a chance?"

"Of course I don't know for sure," Tom added, "but we've got to go by signs - just like Indian signs along a trail. If you pick up an old flint arrowhead you know you're on an Indian trail."

"Christopherr *Columbus!* But I'd like to find one of those arrowheads now!" said Archer.

# CHAPTER XVI

## THE WEAVER OF MERNON

But for all these fine deductions, you are not to suppose that Tom and Archer approached the little house without trepidation. The nearer they came to it the less dependable seemed Tom's theory.

"It might be all right in a story book," Archer said, backsliding into dismal apprehensions. But before he had a chance to lose his courage Tom had knocked softly on the door. They could hear a scuffling sound inside and then the door was opened cautiously by a little stooping old man with a pale, deeply wrinkled face, and long, straight white hair. From his ragged peasant's attire he must have been very poor and the primitive furnishings in the dimly lighted room, of which they caught a glimpse, confirmed this impression. But he had a pair of keen blue eyes which scrutinized the travellers rather tremulously, evidently supposing them to be German soldiers.

"What have I done?" he asked fearfully in German.

Tom wasted no time trying to understand him, but bringing forth his iron button he held it out silently.

The effect was electrical; the old man clutched the button eagerly and poured forth a torrent of French as he dragged the boys one after the other into his poor abode and shut the door.

"We're Americans," said Tom. "We can't understand."

"It iss all ze same," said the man. "I will talk in ze American. How you came with ziss button - yess? Who have sent you?"

To Tom's surprise he spoke English better than either Florette or her brother, and the boys were infinitely grateful and relieved to hear their own language spoken in this remote place.

"We are Americans," said Tom. "We escaped from the prison camp across the Alsace border, and we're on our way to the frontier. I knew you were French on account of the fleur-de-lis on the end of your flagpole -"

"And ze button - yess?" the old man urged, interrupting him.

Tom told him the whole story of Frenchy and the Leteurs, and of how he had come by his little talisman.

"I have fought in zat regiment," the old man said, "many years before you are born. I have seen Alsace lost - yess. If you were Germans I would *die* before I would give you food. But I make you true welcome. I have been many years in America. Ah, I have surprise you."

"What is this place?" Archer ventured to ask.

"Ziss is Mernon - out of fifty-two men they take forty-one to ze trenches. My two sons, who are weavers too, they must go. Now they take the women and the young girls."

Further conversation developed the fact that the old man had worked in a silk mill in America for many years and had returned to Alsace and this humble place of his birth only after both of his sons, who like himself were weavers, had been forced into the German service. "If I do not come back and claim my home, it is gone," he said. So he had returned and was working the old hand loom with his aged fingers, here in the place of his birth.

He was greatly interested in the boys' story and gave them freely of his poor store of food which they ate with a relish. Apparently he was not under the cloud of suspicion or perhaps his age and humble condition and the obscurity and remoteness of his dwelling gave him a certain immunity. In any event, he carried his loathing of the Germans with a fine independence.

"In America," he said, "ze people do not know about ziss - ziss beast. Here we *know*. Here in little Mernon our women must work to make ze road down to ze river. Why is zere needed a road to ze river? Why is zere needed ze new road above Basel? To bring back so many prisoners - wounded? Bah! Ziss is what zey *say*. Lies! I have been a soldier. Eighty-two years I am old. And much I have travelled. So can I see. What you say in Amerique - make two and two together - yess? Zere will be tramping of soldiers over zese roads to invade little Switzerland. Am I right? If it is necessaire - yess! *Necessaire!* Faugh!"

This was the first open statement the boys had heard as to the new roads, all of which converged suspiciously in the direction of the Swiss frontier. They were for bringing home German wounded; they were to facilitate internal communication; they were for this, that and the other useful and innocent purpose, but they all ran toward the Swiss border or to some highway which ran thither.

"Ziss is ze last card they have to play - to stab little Switzerland in ze back and break through," the old man said. "In ze south runs a road from ze trench line across to ze Rhine. Near zere I have an old comrade - Blondel. Togezzer we fight side by side, like brothers. When ze boat comes, many times he comes to see me. Ze last time he come he tell me how ze new road goes past his house - all women and young girls working. It comes from ziss other road zat goes from ze trenches over to ze Rhine. South it goes - you see?" he added shrewdly. "So now if you are so clevaire to see a fleur-de-lis where none is intentioned, so zen you can tell, maybe, why will zey build a road zat goes south?"

Tom, fascinated by the old man's sagacity and vehemence, only shook his head.

"Ah, you are not so clevaire to suspect! Ziss is Amerique! Nevaire will she suspect."

Tom did not altogether like this reference to Uncle Sam's gullibility, but he contented himself with believing that it was meant as a thing of the past.

"They can't flim-flam us now," Archer ventured.

"Flam-flim - no," the old man said, with great fervor.

"Maybe that's where they took my friend's sister and his mother," Tom said.

"I will tell you vere zey take them," the old man interrupted. "You know Alsace - no? So! See! I tell you." He approached, poking Tom's chest with his bony finger and screwing up his blue eyes until he seemed a very demon of shrewdness. They wondered if he were altogether sane.

"Nuzzing can zey hide from Melotte," he went on. "Far south, near Basel, zere lives my comrade - Blondel. To him must you show your button - yess. In Norne he lives."

"We'll write that down," said Tom.

"Nuzzing you write down," the old man said sharply, clutching Tom's arm. "In your brain where you are so clevaire - zere you write it. So! You are not so clevaire as Melotte. Now I will show you how you shall find Mam'selle," he went on with a sly wink.

Emptying some wool out of a paper bag, he pressed the wrinkles from the bag with his trembling old hand and bending over the rough table close to the lantern, he drew a map somewhat similar to, though less complete than, the one given here.

There is nothing like a map to show one "where he is at," to quote Archer's phrase, and the boys followed with great interest as Melotte penciled the course of the Rhine and the places which he wished to emphasize in the southern part of Alsace.

"Here at Norne lives my comrade, Blondel," he said. "Two years we work togezzer at Pas*sake* - you know? In ze great silk mills."

"Passaic," said Tom; "that's near Bridgeboro, where I live."

"Pas*sake*, yess. So now you are so clevaire to know who shall leeve in a house, I will tell you how you shall know ze house of my comrade, Blondel. *By ze blue flag with one black spot!* Yess? You know what ziss shall be? *Billet!*" He gave Archer a dig in the ribs as if this represented the high water mark of sagacity.

"Oh, I know," said Archer; "it means Gerrman officerrs are billeted therre. Go-o-od *night!* Not for us!"

The old man did not seem quite to understand, but he turned again to his map. "Here now is ze new road," he said, drawing it with his shaky old hand. "From ze Rhine road it runs - south - so. Now you are so clevaire - Yankee clevaire, ha, ha, ha!" he laughed with a kind of irritating hilarity; "why should zey make ziss road? From ze north - from Leteur - all around - zey bring our women to make ziss road. Ziss is where Mam'selle is - so! Close by it lives my comrade, Blondel. Ziss is noble army to command, ugh!" He gritted his teeth. "*All are women!*"

Tom looked at the map, as old Melotte poised his skinny finger above it and peered eagerly up into his face from the depths of his scraggly white hair. It was little enough Tom knew about military affairs and he thought that this lonesome old weaver was in his dotage. But surely this new road could be for but one purpose, and that was the quick transfer of troops from the Alsatian front to the Swiss border. And the sudden conscription of women and girls for the making of the road seemed plausible enough. Could it be that this furnished a clew to the whereabouts of Florette Leteur? And if it did, what hope was there of reaching her, or of rescuing her?

He listened only abstractedly to the old man's rambling talk of Germany's intention to violate Swiss neutrality if that became necessary to her purpose. His eyes were half closed as he looked at the rough sketch and he saw there considerably more than old Melotte had drawn.

He saw Frenchy's sister Florette, slender and frail, wielding some heavy implement, doing her enforced bit in this work of shameless betrayal. He could see her eyes, sorrow-laden and filled with fear. He could see her as she had stood talking with him that night in the arbor. He could see her, orphaned and homeless, slaving under the menacing shadow of a German officer who sprawled and lorded it in the poor home of this Blondel close by the new road. *Here he climb to drop ze grapes down my neck. Bad boy!* Strange, how that particular phrase of hers singled itself out and stuck in his memory.

"So now you are so *clevaire*," he half heard old Melotte saying to Archer.

And Tom Slade said nothing, only thought, and thought, and thought....

# CHAPTER XVII

## THE CLOUDS GATHER

"We never thought about asking him to translate that letterr," said Archer.

"I'm not thinking about that letter," Tom answered. "All I'm thinking about now is what he said about that new road. I'm not even thinking about their going through Switzerland, either," he added with great candor. "I'm thinking about Frenchy's sister. If they've got her working there I'm going to rescue her. I made up my mind to that."

"*Some job!*" commented Archer.

"It don't make any difference how much of a job it is," said Tom, with that set look about his mouth that Archer was coming to know and respect.

They were clambering up the hillside again, for not all old Melotte's hospitable urging could induce Tom to remain in the hut until daylight.

He would have liked to take along the rough sketch which the old man had made, but this Melotte had strenuously opposed, saying that no maps should be carried by strangers in Germany. So Tom had to content himself with the old man's rather rambling directions.

Percy Keese Fitzhugh

Several things remained indelibly impressed on his mind. Old Melotte had told him that upon the western bank of the Rhine about fifteen miles above the Swiss border was an old gray castle with three turrets, and that directly opposite this and not far from the Alsatian bank was the little village of Norne.

"The way I make it out," said Archer, "is that this Blondel, whoeverr he is, has got some Gerrman officerr wished on him and that geezerr has charrge of the women worrking on the new road. I'd like to know how you expect to get within a mile of those people in the daytime."

"We got plenty of time to think it out," Tom answered doggedly, "'cause we'll be in the woods a couple of days and nights and that's where thoughts come to you."

"We'd be big fools, afterr gettin' all the way down to the frontierr to cross the riverr and go huntin' forr a road in broad daylight," said Archer; "we'd only get caught."

"Well, we'll get caught then," retorted Tom.

"Anyway, I think the old fellow's half crazy," Archer persisted. "He's got roads on the brain. He jumps all around from Norrne to Passaic and -"

"He gave us something to eat," said Tom curtly.

"Well, I didn't say he didn't, did I?" Archer snapped. "If we'd had any sense, we'd have stayed therre all night like he wanted us to. Therre wouldn't have been any dangerr in that old shack, a hundred miles from nowherre."

"We're safest in the hills," said Tom.

"It's going to rain, too," Archer grumbled.

Tom made no answer and they scrambled in silence up the uninviting hillside, till old Melotte's shack could be seen far below with the dim light in its windows.

"You'rre so particularr about not bein' caught," Archer began again, "it's a wonder you wouldn't think morre about that when we get down close to the borrderr. If I've got to be caught at all I'd ratherr be caught now."

They had regained the height above the little hamlet and to the south they could see the clustering lights of Strassbourg and here and there a moving light upon the river.

"We've got to cross that, too, I s'pose," Archer said sulkily.

Tom did not answer. The plain fact was that they were both thoroughly tired out, with that dog-tiredness which comes suddenly as a reaction after days of nerve-racking apprehension and hard physical effort. For the first two days their nervous excitement had kept them up. But now they were fagged and the tempting invitation to remain at the hovel had been too strong for Archer. Moreover, this new scheme of Tom's to divert their course in a hazardous quest for Florette Leteur was not at all to his liking. But mostly he was tired and everything looks worse when one is tired.

"We're not going to keep on hiking it tonight, are we?" he demanded.

"You said yourself that the old man was kind of - a little off, like," Tom answered patiently. "He's got the bug that he's very shrewd and that he can always get the best of the Germans. Do you think I'd take a chance staying there? We took a chance as it was."

"Yes, and you'rre going to take a biggerr one if you go chasing all over Gerrmany after that girrl. You won't find herr. That was a lot of rattlebrain talk anyway - we're *so clevaire!*"

"There's no use making fun of him," said Tom; "he helped us."

Percy Keese Fitzhugh

"We'll get caught, that'll be the end of it," said Archer sullenly. Tom did not answer.

"You seem to be the boss of everything, anyway."

They scrambled diagonally down the eastern slope of the high ground, heading always toward the river and after an hour's travelling came out upon its shore.

"Here's where we'll have to cross if we're going to cross at all," said Tom. "What do you say?"

"*I* haven't got anything to say," said Archer; "*you're* doin' all the saying."

"If we go any farther south," Tom went on patiently, "we'll be too near Strassbourg and we're likely to meet boats. Listen."

From across the river came the spent whistle of a locomotive accompanied by the rattling of a hurrying train, the steady sound, thin and clear in the still night, mingling with its own echoes. A few lights, widely separated, were visible across the water and one, high up, reassured Tom that the mountains, the foothills of which they had followed, continued at no great distance from the opposite shore.

There were welcoming fastnesses over there, he knew, and a dim, wide belt of forest extending southward. There, safe from the haunts of men, or at least with timely warning of any hamlets nestling in those sombre depths, he and his comrade might press southward toward that promised land, the Swiss border.

Yet, strangely enough (for one side of a river is pretty much like the other) Tom felt a certain regret at the thought of leaving Alsace. Perhaps his memory of the Leteurs had something to do with this. Perhaps he had just the boyish feeling that it would change their luck. And he knew that over there he would be truly in the enemy's country, with the magic of his little talisman vanished in air.

Yet right here he must decide between open roads and stealthy hospitality and that silent, embracing hospitality which the lonesome heights would offer. And he decided in favor of the lonesome heights. Perhaps after all it was not the enemy's country, though the names of Baden and Schwarzwald certainly had a hostile sound.

But the rugged mountains and dim woods are never enemies of the scout, and perhaps Tom Slade of Temple Camp felt that even the Schwarzwald, which is the Black Forest, would forget its allegiance to whisper its secrets in his ear.

Percy Keese Fitzhugh

# CHAPTER XVIII

## IN THE RHINE

"What do you say?" said Tom. "It's up to both of us."

"Oh, don't mind me," Archer answered sarcastically. "*I* don't count. I know one thing - *I'm* going to head straight for the Swiss borderr. If crossing the river herre's the quickest way to do it, then that's what I'm going to do, you can bet!"

For a moment Tom did not speak, then looking straight at Archer, he said, -

"You don't forget how she helped us, do you?"

"I'm not saying anything about that," said Archer. "My duty's to Uncle Sam. You've got the *crazy* notion now that you want to rescue a girrl, just like fellerrs do in story books. If you'rre going to be thinking about herr all the time I might as well go by myself. I could get along all right, if it comes to that."

"Well, I couldn't," said Tom, with a note of earnestness in his voice. "Anyway, there's no use of our scrapping about it 'cause I don't suppose we'll find her. As long as we're going south through the mountains we might as well see if we can pick out Norne with the glass. Maybe we could even see that feller Blondel's house. The old man said the west slopes of the mountains were steep and that they run close to the river down there, so we ought to be able to pick out Norne with the glass.

There isn't any harm in that, is there?" he added conciliatingly, "as long as we've got the glass?"

Archer maintained a sullen silence.

"I know we've got to think about Uncle Sam, and I know you're patriotic," said Tom generously, "and we can't afford to be taking big chances. But if you had known her brother, you'd feel the way I do - that's one sure thing."

"I wouldn't run the risk of getting pinched and sent back to prison just on account of a girrl," said Archer scornfully. "*That's one sure thing*," he added, sulkily mimicking Tom's phrase.

"That ain't the way it is," said Tom, flushing a little. "I ain't - if that's what you mean. Anyway, I admit we got to be careful, and I promise you if we can't spy out the house and the road with the glass I won't cross the river again till we get to the border."

"First thing you know somebody'll come along if we keep on standing here," said Archer.

"Here, you take one of these rubber gloves," said Tom. "Shut the glass and see if it'll go inside. I'll put the flashlight and the compass in the other one. It's going to rain, too. Here, let me do it," he added rather tactlessly, as he closed the little telescope and forced its smaller end down into the longest of the big glove fingers. "Twist the top of it and turn the edges over, see?" he added, doing it himself, "and it's watertight. I can make a watertight stopple for a bottle with a long strip of paper, but you got to know how to wind it," he added, with clumsy disregard of his companion's mood. Tom was a hopeless bungler in some ways.

"Oh, surre, *you* can do anything," said Archer.

"Maybe it would be best if you held it in your teeth," said

Tom thoughtfully; "unless you can swim with it in your hand."

The compass and the flashlight, which indeed were more susceptible of damage from the water than the precious glass, were encased in the other rubber glove, and the two fugitives waded out into the black, silent river.

Scarcely had their feet left the bottom when the first drop of rain fell upon Tom's head, and a chill gust of wind caught him and bore him a yard or two out of his course. He spluttered and looked about for Archer, but could see nothing in the darkness. He did not want to call for he knew how far voices carry across the water, and though the spot was isolated he would take no chances.

It rained hard and the wind, rising to a gale, lashed the black water into whitecaps. Tom strove vainly to make headway against the storm, but felt himself carried, willy-nilly, he knew not where. He tried to distinguish the light beyond the Baden shore, which he had selected for a beacon, but he could not find it. At last he called to Archer.

"I'm going to turn back," he said; "come on - are you all right?"

If Archer answered his voice was drowned by the wind and rain. For a few moments Tom struggled against the elements, hoping to regain the Alsatian shore. His one guiding instinct in all the hubbub was the conviction that the wind smelled like an east wind and that it ought to carry him back to the nearer shore. He would have given a good deal for a glimpse of his precious little compass now.

"Where are you?" he called again. "The light's gone. Let the wind carry you back - it's east."

He could hear no answer save the mocking wind and the breaking of the water. This latter sound made him think the shore was not far distant. But when, after a few moments, he did not feel the bottom, his heart sank. He had been lost in the woods and as a tenderfoot he had known the feeling of panic despair. And he had been in the ocean and seen his ship go down with a torpedo's jagged rent in her side. But he had never been lost in the water in the sense of losing all his bearings in the darkness. For a minute it quite unnerved him and his stout heart sank within him.

Then out of the tumult came a thin, spent voice, barely audible and seeming a part of the troubled voices of the night.

"- lost - ," it said; " - going down -"

Tom listened eagerly, his heart still, his blood cold within him.

"Keep calling," he answered, "so I'll know where you are. I'll get to you all right - keep your nerve."

He listened keenly, ready to challenge the force of the storm with all his young skill and strength, and thinking of naught else now. But no guiding voice answered.

Could he have heard aright? Surely, there was no mistaking. It was a human voice that had spoken and whatever else it had said that one, tragic word had been clearly audible:

"- down -"

Archer had gone down.

# CHAPTER XIX

## TOM LOSES HIS FIRST CONFLICT
## WITH THE ENEMY

"Down!"

For the first time in Tom Slade's life a sensation of utter despair gripped him and it was not until several seconds had elapsed, while he was tossed at the mercy of the storm, that he was able to get a grip on himself. He struck out frantically and for just a brief minute was guilty of a failing which he had never yielded to - the perilous weakness of being rattled and hitting hard at nothing. In swimming, above all things, this is futile and dangerous, and presently Tom regained his mental poise and struck out calmly, swimming in the direction in which the wind bore him, for there was nothing else to do. Not that his effort helped him much, but he knew the good rule that one should never be passive in a crisis, for inaction is as depressing to the spirit as frantic exertion is to the body. And he knew that by swimming he could keep his "morale" - a word which he had heard a good deal lately.

His heart was sick within him and a kind of cold desperation seized him. Archer, whom he had known away back home in America, whom he had found by chance in the German prison camp, who had trudged over the hills and through the woods with him, was lost. He would never see him again. Archer, who was always after souvenirs....

These were not thoughts exactly, but they flitted through Tom's consciousness as he struggled to keep his head clear of the tempestuous waters. And even in his own desperate plight he recalled that their last words had been words of discord, for he knew now (generous as he was) that *he* was to blame for this dreadful end of all their fine hopes - that Archer had been right - they should have stayed at Melotte's hovel. Amid the swirl of the waters, as he swam he knew not where, he remembered how Archer had said he ought to think of his duty to Uncle Sam and not imperil his chance to help by going after Florette Leteur.

He was sick, utterly sick, and nearer to hopelessness than he had ever been in his life; but he struck out in a kind of mechanical resignation, believing that the wind and the trend of the water must bring him to one shore or the other before he was exhausted. There was no light anywhere, no clew or beacon of any sort in that wild blackness, and since he therefore had no reason to oppose his strength to the force of the storm he swam steadily in the direction in which it carried him. It made no difference. Nothing mattered now....

After a while the noise of the lashing changed to that lapping sound which only contact with the land can give, and soon Tom could distinguish a solid mass outlined in the hollow blackness of the night. He had no guess whether it was the Baden or the Alsatian shore that he was approaching nor how far north or south he had been carried. Nor did he much care.

His foot touched something hard which brought him to the realization that he must lessen the force of his advance or perhaps have his life dashed out upon a rocky shore; and presently he was staggering forward, brushing his hair away from his eyes, wondering where he was, and scarcely sensible of anything - his head throbbing, his whole body on the verge of exhaustion.

"It's my fault - anyway - I got to admit it -" he thought, "and - it serves - me - right."

One firm resolution came to him. Now that Providence had seen fit to cast him ashore, if he was to be permitted to continue his flight alone, he would go straight for his goal, the Swiss border, and not be led astray (that is what he called it, *led astray*) by any other enterprise. His duty as a soldier, and he thought of himself as a soldier now, was clear. His business was to help Uncle Sam win the war and he must leave it to Uncle Sam to put an end to the stealing of young girls and to restore them to their homes. He saw himself now, as Archer had depicted him, in the silly role of a "story book hero" and he felt ashamed. He knew that General Pershing would not have sent him rescuing girls, and that the best way he could help France, and even the Leteurs, was to hurry up and get into the trenches where he belonged. Yes, Archer was right. And with a pang of remorse Tom remembered how Archer had said it, "rescuing a girrl!" He would never hear Archer talk like that any more....

He had more than once been close enough to death to learn to keep his nerve in the presence of it, but the loss of his companion quite unnerved him. It had not occurred to him that anything *could* happen to Archer, who claimed himself that he always landed right side up because he was lucky. Tom could not realize that he was gone.

Still, comrades were lost to each other every day in that far-flung trench line and in that bloody sea of northern France friends were parted and many went down.

"*Down -*"

How that awful word had sounded - long drawn out and faint in the storm and darkness!

He stumbled over a rocky space and ran plunk into something solid. As he looked up he could distinguish the top of it; uneven and ragged it seemed against the blackness of the night. Whatever it was, it seemed to be slender and rather high, and the odd thought came to him that he was on the deck of some mammoth submarine, looking up at the huge conning tower. Perhaps it was because he *had* once been rescued by a submarine, or perhaps just because his wits were uncertain and his nerves unstrung, but it was fully a minute before he realized that he was on solid earth - or rock. It afforded him a measure of relief.

What that grim black thing could be that frowned upon him he did not know, and he staggered around it, feeling it with his hands. It was of masonry and presently he came to what was evidently a door, which opened as he leaned against it. Its silent hospitality was not agreeable to him; the very thought of a possible German habitation roused him out of his fatigue and despair, and with a sudden quick instinct he drew stealthily back until presently he felt the water lapping his feet again.

Here, at a comparatively safe distance, he paused for breath after what he felt to be a worse peril than the storm, and felt for the one trusty friend he had left - the little compass. The precious rubber glove containing this and the flashlight was safe in his pocket, and he held both under his coat and tried to throw the light upon the compass and get his bearings. But the glove must have leaked, for the battery was dead. The little compass, which was to prove so useful in days to come, was probably still loyal after its immersion, but he could not distinguish the dial clearly.

He knew he must go southeast, where the dim woods seemed now to beckon him like a living mother. Never had the thought of the mountains and the lonely forest been so grateful to this scout before. If only he had strength to get there....

"What you *got* to do - you do," he panted slowly under his breath, frowning at the compass and trying in the darkness to see which way that faithful little needle turned. Once, twice, he looked fearfully up toward that grim building.

Then he decided, as best he might, which direction was

southeast and dragged his aching legs that way until presently he was stumbling in the water again.

Surely, he thought, the river ran almost north and south, and southeast *must* lead on into the mountains. But perhaps he had not read the compass aright or perhaps he was on the edge of a deep bay, which would mean water extending still westward. Or perhaps he was on the Alsatian shore.

For a moment he stood bewildered. Then he tried to read the compass again and started forward in the direction which he thought to be west. If he were on the Alsatian shore, this should take him away from that black, heartless Teuton ruin.

But it only took him into a chaos of broken, shiny rock where he stumbled and fell, cutting his knee and making his head throb cruelly.

And then Tom Slade, seeing that fate was against him, and having used all the resource and young strength that he had, to get to the boys "over there," gave up and lay among the jagged rocks, holding his head with one bruised hand and thinking hopelessly of this end of all his efforts.

# CHAPTER XX

## A NEW DANGER

He did not know how long he lay there, but after a while he crept along over the slimy rocks and because it was not easy to stand alone he limped to that grim, threatening structure, and leaned against it, trying to collect his faculties.

"If he was - only here now," he breathed, half aloud, "I'd let him - I'd be willing not to be boss - like he said. That's the - trouble - with me - I'm always wanting to - be  - Oh, my head -"

He knew now, what it was a pretty hard thing for one of his indomitable temperament to realize, that things were out of his hands, that he could go no farther. North or south or east or west, he could go no farther. Capture or firing squad or starvation and death from exhaustion, he could go no farther. His name would not be sent home on the casualty lists, any more than Archer's would, but they had *tried*, and done their bit as well as they could.

There was one faint hope left; perhaps this house was not occupied, or if it was on the Alsatian side of that terrible river (a true Hun river, if there ever was one) it might be occupied by a Frenchman. Scarcely knowing what he was doing, Tom pushed the door open and staggered inside. Dazed and suffering as he was, he was conscious of the rain pelting on the roof above him and sounding more audibly than outside where the boisterous river drowned the sound of the downpour.

Something big and soft which caught in his feet was directly before him and he stumbled and fell upon it. And there he lay, pressing his throbbing forehead, which seemed bursting with fresh pain from the force of his fall.

He had a reckless impulse to end all doubt by calling aloud in utter abandonment. But this impulse passed, perhaps because he did not have the strength or spirit to call.

Soon, from mere exhaustion, he fell into a fitful, feverish slumber accompanied by a nightmare in which the lashing of the wind and rain outside were conjured into the clangor and hoof beats of cavalry and he was hopelessly enmeshed in a barbed-wire entanglement.

With the first light of dawn he saw that he was lying upon a mass of fishnet and that his feet and arms were entangled in its meshes.

He was in a small, circular apartment with walls of masonry and a broken spiral stairway leading up to a landing beside a narrow window. Rain streamed down from this window and trickled in black rivulets all over the walls. A very narrow doorway opened out of this circular room, from which the door was broken away, leaving two massive wrought-iron hinges sticking out conspicuously into the open space. As Tom's eyes fell upon these he thought wistfully of how eagerly Archer would have appropriated one of them as a "souveneerr." Poor, happy-go-lucky Archer!

"I thought he was a good swimmer," Tom thought, "because he lived so near Black Lake.[A] It was all my fault. He probably just didn't like to say he wasn't -"

[Footnote A: The lake on the shore of which Temple Camp was situated.]

He closed his eyes for a moment, trying to ease the pain in his head and collect his scattered senses. Evidently, he was alone in this dank place, for there was no sign of occupancy nor any sound but the light patter of rain without, for the storm had spent its fury and subsided into a steady drizzle.

He dragged himself to his feet, and though his knee was stiff he was glad to discover that he was not incapable of walking. He believed he was not feverish now and that his headache was caused by shock and bruising rather than by illness. Perhaps, he thought, he was not so badly off after all. Except for Archer....

Limping to the doorway he peered cautiously out. The sky was dull and hazy and a steady, drizzling rain fell. There is something about a drear, rainy day which "gets" one, if he has but a makeshift shelter; and this bleak, gray morning carried poor Tom's mind back with a rush to rainy days at his beloved Temple Camp when scouts were wont to gather in tent and cabin for yarns.

He now saw that he was on a little rocky islet in the middle of the river and that the structure which had sheltered him was a small tower, very much like a lighthouse except that it was not surmounted by a light, having instead that rough turret coping familiar in medieval architecture. Far off, through the haze, he could distinguish, close to the shore, a gray castle with turrets, which from his compass he knew to be on the Baden side. He thought he could make out a road close to the shore, and other houses, and he wished that he had the spy-glass so that he might study this locality which he hoped to pass through.

Of course, he no longer cherished any hope of finding Florette Leteur; Archer's chiding words still lingered in his mind, and, moreover, without the glass he could do nothing for he certainly would never have thought of entering Norne without first "piking" it from a safe vantage point.

There was nothing to do now but nurse his swollen knee and

rest, in the hope that by night he would be able to swim to the Baden shore and get into the hills. Never before had he so longed for the forest.

"If it wasn't for - for him being lost," he told himself, as he limped back into the tower, "I wouldn't be so bad off. There's nobody lives here, that's sure. Maybe fishermen come here, but nobody'll come today, I'll bet."

After all, luck had not been unqualifiedly against him, he thought. Here he was in an isolated spot in the wide river. What was the purpose of this little tower on its pile of rocks he could not imagine, but it was fast going to ruin and save for the rotting fishing seine there was no sign of human occupancy.

If only Archer were there it would not be half bad. But the thought of his companion's loss sickened him and robbed the lonely spot of such aspect of security as it might otherwise have had for him. Still, he must go on, he must reach the boys in France, and fight for Archer too, now - Archer, whom his own blundering had consigned to death in these treacherous waters....

He looked out again through the doorway at the dull sky, and the rain falling steadily upon the sullen water. It was a day to chill one's spirit and sap one's courage. The whole world looked gray and cheerless. Again, as on the night before, he heard the rattle of a train in the distance. High up through the drenched murky air, a bird sped across the river, and somehow its disappearance among the hills left Tom with a sinking feeling of utter desolation. In Temple Camp, on a day like this, they would be in Roy Blakeley's tent, telling stories....

"Anyway, it's better to be alone than in some German's house," he tried to cheer himself. "We - I - kept away from 'em so far, anyway -"

He stopped, holding his breath, with every muscle tense, and his heart sank within him. For out of that inner doorway came a sound - a sound unmistakably human - tragically human, it seemed now, shattering his returning courage and leaving him hopeless.

It was the sound of some one coughing!

# CHAPTER XXI

## COMPANY

Ordinarily Tom Slade would have stopped to think and would have kept his nerve and acted cautiously; but he had not sufficiently recovered his poise to meet this emergency wisely. He knew he could not swim away, that capture was now inevitable, and instead of pausing to collect himself he gave way to an impulse which he had never yielded to before, an impulse born of his shaken nerves and stricken hope and the sort of recklessness which comes from despair. What did it matter? Fate was against him....

With a kind of defiant abandonment he limped to the little stone doorway and stood there like an apparition, clutching the sides with trembling hands. But whatever reckless words of surrender he meant to offer froze upon his lips, and he swayed in the opening, staring like a madman.

For reclining upon a rough bunk, with knees drawn up, was Archibald Archer, busily engaged in whittling a stick, his freckled nose wrinkling up in a kind of grotesque accompaniment to each movement of his hand against the hard wood.

"I - I thought -" Tom began.

"Well, - I'll - be -" countered Archer.

For a moment they stared at each other in blank amaze. Then

a smile crept over Tom's face, a smile quite as unusual with him as his sudden spirit of surrender had been; a smile of childish happiness. He almost broke out laughing from the reaction.

"Are you carvin' a souvenir?" he said foolishly.

"No, I ain't carrvin' no souveneerr," Archer answered. "Therre's fish among those rocks and I'm goin' to spearr 'em."

"You ain't carvin' a *what*!" said Tom.

"I ain't carrvin' a souveneerr," Archer said with the familiar Catskill Mountain roll to his R's.

"I just wanted to hear you say it," said Tom, limping over to him and for the first time in his life yielding to the weakness of showing sentiment.

"All night long," he said, sitting down on the edge of the bunk, "I was thinkin' how you said it - and it sounds kind of good -"

"How'd you make out in the riverr?" Archer asked.

"You can't even say *river*," said Tom, laughing foolishly in his great relief.

"It was some storrm, all right! But I got the matches safe anyway, and they'll strike, 'cause I tried one."

"You ought to have made a whisk stick[A] to try it," said Tom, then caught himself up suddenly. "But I ain't going to tell you what you ought to do any more. I'm goin' to stop bossin'."

[Footnote A: A stick the end of which is separated into fine shavings which readily catch the smallest flame, a familiar device used by scouts.]

"I got yourr spy-glass forr you," said Archer. "I had to dive f'rr't. Didn't you hearr me call to you it was lost and I was goin' down f'rr't?"

"-lost - down -"

The tragic words flitted again through Tom's mind, and he reached out and took Archer's hand hesitatingly as if ashamed of the feeling it implied.

"What'd you do that for? You were a fool," he said.

"What you *got* to do, you do," said Archer; "that's what you'rre always sayin'. Didn't you say you wanted it so's you could see that fellerr Blondel's house from the mountains? Therre it is," he said, nodding toward an old ring-net that stood near, "and it's some souveneerr too, 'cause it's been at the bottom of the old Rhine."

Tom looked at the spy-glass which Archer had thrown into the net and the net seemed all hazy and tangled for his eyes were brimming. He would not spare himself now.

"I see I'm the fool," he stammered; "I thought I shouldn't have started across because maybe you couldn't swim so good and didn't want to admit it."

"Me? I dived in Black Lake before you werre borrn," said Archer. This was not quite true, since he was two years younger than Tom, but Tom only smiled at him through glistening eyes.

"I see now I was crazy to think about finding her - anyway -"

"You haven't forrgot how she treated us, have you?" Archer retorted, quoting Tom's own words. "It came to me all of a sudden, when I dropped the glove, and that's when I called to you. And all of a sudden I thought how you walked back toward the house with herr that night and - and - do you think I don't understand - you darrned big chump?"

# CHAPTER XXII

## BREAKFAST WITHOUT FOOD CARDS

"Do you know what I think?" said Archer. "If Alsace used to belong to France, then the Rhine must have been the boundary between France and Gerrmany and we'rre right on that old frontierr now - hey? I'm a smarrt lad, huh? They used to have watch towers and things 'cause I got kept in school once forr sayin' a poem wrong about a fellerr that was in a watch towerr on the Rhine. I bet this towerr had something to do with that old frontierr and I bet it was connected with that castle overr on shorre, too. Therre was a picture of a fellerr in a kind of an arrmorr looking off the top of a towerr just like this - I remember 'cause I marrked him up with a pencil so's he'd have a swallerr-tailed coat and a sunbonnet."

Archer's education was certainly helping him greatly.

"If we could once get overr therre into that Black Forest," he continued, scanning the Baden shore and the heights beyond with the rescued glass, "we'd be on easy street 'cause I remember gettin' licked forr sayin', 'the abrupt west slopes of this romantic region are something or otherr with wild vineyards that grow in furious thing-um-bobs -'"

"*What?*" said Tom.

"*Anyway*, there's lots of grapes there," Archer concluded.

Percy Keese Fitzhugh

"If that's the way you said it I don't blame 'em for lickin' you," said sober Tom. "I think by tonight I'll be able to swim it. There seems to be some houses over there - that's one thing I don't like."

The Baden side, as well as they could make out through the haze, was pretty thickly populated for a mile or two, but the lonesome mountains arose beyond and once there, they would be safe, they felt sure.

They spent the day in the dilapidated frontier tower, as Archer called it, and he was probably not far from right in his guess about it. Certainly it had not been used for many years except apparently by fishermen occasionally, and the rotten condition of the seines showed that even such visitors had long since ceased to use it. Perhaps indeed it was a sort of outpost watch tower belonging to the gray castle which they saw through the mist.

"Maybe it belonged to a Gerrman baron," suggested Tom.

"Anyway, it's a *barren* island," said Archer; "are you hungry?"

Tom sat in the doorway, favoring his hurt knee, and watched Archer move cautiously about among the sharp, slippery rocks, where he succeeded in cornering and spearing several bewildered fish which the troubled waters of the night had marooned in these small recesses.

"I'm afraid, you'll be seen from the shore," Tom said, but without that note of assurance and authority which he had been accustomed to use.

"Don't worry," said Archer, "it's too thick and hazy. Just wait till I spearr one morre. Therre's a beaut, now -"

They wasted half a dozen damp matches before they could get flame enough to ignite the whisk stick which Tom held ready, but when they succeeded they "commandeered" the broken door as a "warr measurre," to quote Archer, and kindled a fire just inside the doorway where they believed that the smoke, mingling with the mist, would not be seen through the gray, murky atmosphere.

It is a great mistake to be prejudiced against a fish just because it is German. Tom and Archer were quite free from that narrow bias. And if it should ever be your lot to be marooned in a ramshackle old watch tower on the Rhine on a dull, rainy day, remember that the same storm which has marooned you will have marooned some fishes among the crevices of rock - only you must be careful to turn them often and not let them burn. The broken rail of an old spiral stairway, if there happens to be one handy, can be twisted into a rough gridiron, and if you happen to think of it (as Tom did) you can use the battery case of your flashlight for a drinking-cup.

"If we couldn't have managed to get a light with these damp matches," he said, as they partook of their sumptuous breakfast, "we'd have just had to wait till the sun came out and we could a' got one with the lens in the spy-glass."

Once a scout, always a scout!

## CHAPTER XXIII

## THE CATSKILL VOLCANO IN ERUPTION

All day long the dull, drizzling rain continued, and as the hours passed their hope revived and their courage strengthened.

"Therre's one thing I'm glad of," said Archer, "and that's that I thought about putting that Gerrman soldierr's paperrs in the glove. I've got a hunch I'd like to know what that letterr says."

"I'm glad you did," said Tom. "I got to admit *I* didn't think of it."

By evening Tom's knee was much better though still sore, and his head pained not at all. They had but one thought now - to swim to shore and get into the mountains where they believed they could continue their course southward. Swimming to the nearest point on the east, or Baden bank, would, they could see by the glass, bring them into a fairly thickly populated district and how to get past this and into the protecting highlands troubled them. They had thus far avoided civilization and towns, where they knew the ever-watchful eye of Prussian authority was to be feared. They knew well enough that their wet garments constituted no disguise; but they could, at least, get to shore and see how the land lay.

They were greatly elated at their success so far, and at their providential reunion. Whatever difficulties they had encountered they had surmounted, and whatever difficulties lay ahead they would meet and overcome, they felt sure.

As the day wore away, the rain ceased, but the sky remained dull and murky. Their plan was to wait for the darkness and they were talking over their good luck and what they thought the rosy outlook when Tom, looking toward the Alsatian shore with the glass, saw a small boat which was scarcely distinguishable in the hazy twilight.

"I don't believe it's coming this way," he said confidently, handing the glass to Archer. But at the same time he was conscious of a sinking sensation.

"Yes, it is," said Archer; "it's coming right for us."

"Maybe they're just rowing across," said Tom.

Archer watched the boat intently. "It's coming herre all right," he said; "we'rre pinched. Let's get inside, anyway."

Tom smiled with a kind of sickly resignation. "Let's see," he said; "yes, you're right, they've got uniforms, too. It's all up. We might have had sense enough to know. I bet they traced us all the way through Alsace. There's no use trying to beat that crowd," he added in cynical despair.

Hope dashed when it is just reviving brings the most hopeless of all despair, and with Tom, whose nerves had been so shaken, their imminent capture seemed now like a kind of mockery.

"When I found you were all right," he said to Archer in his dull way, "and we were all alone here, I might have known it was too good to be true. I wouldn't bother now. I just got bad luck. - When I tried for the pathfinders' badge and tracked somebody that stole something," he added with his stolid disregard for detail, "I found it was my own father, and I didn't claim the badge. That's the kind of luck *I* got. So I wouldn't try any more. 'Cause if you got bad luck you can't help it. I dropped my knife and the blade stuck in the ground - up at Temple Camp - and that's bad luck. Let 'em come -"

This side of Tom Slade was new to Archer, and he stared curiously at the lowering face of his companion.

"That's what you call losing your morale," he said; "if you lose that - go-od *night*! Suppose General Joffre said that when the Huns werre hitting it forr Paris! S'pose *I* said that when my foot stuck in the mud on the bottom of this plaguey riverr!"

"I didn't know that," said Tom.

"Well, you know it now," retorted Archer, "and I don't give up till they land me back in prison, and I don't give up then, eitherr. And I ain't lettin' any jack-knives get *my* goat - so you can chalk that up in yerr little old noddle!"

"I guess that's the trouble," Tom began; "my head aches -"

"Can you swim now?" Archer demanded.

"You go," said Tom; "my knee's too stiff."

"If you everr say a thing like that to me again," said Archer, his eyes snapping and his freckled face flushing scarlet, "I'll -"

"I didn't think we'd start till midnight," Tom said, "and I thought my knee'd be well enough by that time."

The little boat, as they could see from the doorway, bobbed nearer and nearer and Archer could see that it contained two men.

"They've got on uniforms," Archer said, "but I can't see what they arre. Let's keep inside."

"They know we're here," said Tom; "they'd only shoot us if we started away."

Closer and closer came the little boat until one of its occupants jumped out, hauling it into one of the little rocky caverns of the islet. Then both came striding up to the doorway.

As soon as they caught sight of the boys they paused aghast and seemed to be much more discomfited than either Tom or Archer. Evidently they had not come for the fugitives and the thought occurred to Archer that they might be fugitives themselves.

"Vell, vat you do here, huh?" one asked.

Archer was managing this affair and he managed it in his own sweet way.

"We're herre because we're herre," he said, in a perfect riot of rolling R's.

"You German - no?"

"No, thank goodness! We'rre not," Archer said recklessly. "Are we pinched?"

"How you come here?" the German demanded in that tone of arrogant severity which seems to imply, "I give you and the whole of the rest of the world two seconds to answer."

Tom, whose spirits revived at this rather puzzling turn of affairs, watched the two soldiers keenly and noticed that neither had sword or firearms. And he realized with chagrin that in those few moments of "lost morale," he had been strangely unworthy of himself and of his scout training. And feeling so he let Archer do the talking.

"We're Americans."

"Americans, ach! From prison you escape, huh?" the younger

soldier snapped. "You haff a peekneek here, huh?" And turning to his companion he poured a kind of guttural volley at him, which his comrade answered with a brisk return of heavy verbal fire. Archer, listening intently and using his very rudimentary knowledge of German, gathered that whoever and whatever these two were, they were themselves in the perilous business of escaping.

"They'rre in the same box as we are," he said to Tom. "Don't worry."

It did not occur to the boys then, though they often thought of it afterward, when their acquaintance with the strange race of Huns had been improved, that these two soldiers manifested not the slightest interest in the experiences which the boys had gone through. Almost immediately and without condescending to any discourse with them, the two men fell to discussing how they might *use* them, just as their masters had used Belgium and would use Switzerland and Holland if it fell in with their purpose.

After the generous interest that Frenchy and his people had shown and the lively curiosity about his adventures which British Tommies in the prison camp had displayed, Tom was unable to understand this arrogant disregard. Even a greasy, shifty-eyed Serbian in the prison had asked him about America and "how it felt" to be torpedoed.

It was not just that the two soldiers regarded the boys as enemies, either. They simply were not German and therefore nothing that they did or said counted or was worth talking about.

At last the one who seemed to be the spokesman said, "Ve make a treaty, huh?"

It was more of an announcement than a question, and Archer looked at Tom and laughed.

"A treaty!" said he. "Good *night*! Do you mean a scrap o' paperr?"

"Ve let you off," said the German in a tone of severe condescension. "Ve gif you good clothes - here," he added, seeming unable to get away from his manner of command. "Ve go feeshing. Ve say nutting - ve let you go. You escape - ach, vat iss dis?" he added deprecatingly. "Ve say nutting."

"And we don't say anything eitherr, is that it?" said Archer.

"Eef you talk you can't escape, what? Vy shall you talk, huh?"

Tom looked at Archer, who screwed up his freckled nose and gazed shrewdly at the Germans with a sagacious and highly satisfied look in his mischievous eye.

"That's the treaty, is it?" he said. "And that's just the kind of - shut up!" he interpolated, glancing sideways at Tom. "I'll do the talking - that's just the kind of stuff you'rre trying to put overr on President Wilson, too - tryin' to make the otherr fellerr think he's licked and then making believe you'rre willing to be generous. You got the nerrve (the R's fairly rolled and rumbled as he gathered momentum) - you got the nerrve to come herre with out any guns or sworrds and things and think you can scarre us. Do you know - shut up!" he shot at Tom by way of precaution. "Do you know wherre I think yourr sworrds and things arre? I think the English Tommies have got 'em. I know all about you fellerrs deserrting - I hearrd about it in prison. You'rre deserrting every day. Some of you arre even surrenderrin' to get a good squarre meal. And do you know what an English Tommy told me - you consarrned blufferr, you -"

He was in full swing now, his freckled nose all screwed up and rolling out his R's like artillery. Even sober Tom couldn't help smiling at the good old upstate adjective, *consarrned*.

"He told me a Hun is no good when he loses his gun or his

Percy Keese Fitzhugh

sworrd. You don't think I'm a-scarred of *you*, do you? It's fifty-fifty - two against two, you pair of bloomin' kidnapperrs, and you won't tell 'cause you can't afford to! Same reason as we won't. But you can't put one overr on me any morre'n you can on President Wilson and if you'rre forr making treaties you got to get down off your high horrse - see? You ain't got a superiorrity of numbers now! You got nothing but fourr fists, same as we got. Forr two cents, I'd wash yourr face on those rocks! Treaties! I come from Corrnville Centre, I do, and -"

Tom laughed outright.

"You shut up!" said Archer. "You want to make a treaty, huh? All right, that'll be two Huns less forr the Allies to feed. We'll swap with you, all right, and I wish you luck. I don't know wherre you'rre going or what you'rre going to do and I don't carre a rotten apple. Only you ain't going to dictate terrms to *me*. You'll take these crazy old rags and you'rre welcome to 'em, and we'll take yourr uniforms if that's what you want. Treaty! *We'll* make a treaty with you! And we'll take the boat too, and if that don't satisfy you then that's the end of the what-d'-you-call it! You keep still!" he added, turning to Tom.

# CHAPTER XXIV

## MILITARY ETIQUETTE

"What did you mean by the *what-d'-you call it?*" Tom asked, as they rowed through the darkness for the Baden shore.

"Arrmis-stice," said Archer, wrestling with the word.

"Oh," said Tom.

"That's the way to handle 'em," Archer said with undisguised satisfaction.

"I never saw you like that before," said Tom. "I had to laugh when you said *consarn*."

"That's the Huns all overr," said Archer, his vehemence not yet altogether abated. "They'll try to do the bossing even afterr they'rre licked. Treaties! They've got theirr firrst taste of a *Yankee* treaty, hey? Didn't even have a sworrd and wanted me to think they werre doin' us a favorr! President Wilson knows how to handle that bunch, all right, all right! - Don't row if you'rre tirred."

"It don't hurt my leg to row, only I see now I couldn't swim it."

"Think I didn't know that?" said Archer.

"I got to admit you did fine," said Tom.

"You got to get 'em down on theirr knees beforre you make a treaty with 'em," boasted Archer. "You can see yourself they'rre no good when they haven't got any commanderr - or any arrms. When Uncle Sam makes a treaty with that gang, crabapples, but I hope he gets the boat, too."

"I know what you mean," said Tom soberly. "I have to laugh at the way you talk when you get mad. It reminds me of the country and Temple Camp."

"That's one thing I learned from knockin' around in Europe since this warr starrted," said Archer. "The botches, or whatever you call 'em, are no darrned good when you get 'em alone. The officers may be all right, but the soldierrs are thick. If I couldn't 'a' knocked the bluff out o' that lord-high critturr, I'd 'a' rubbed his pie face in the mud!"

Tom laughed at his homely expletives and Archer broke out laughing too, at his own expense. But for all that, Tom was destined to recall, and that very soon, what Archer had said about the Huns. And he was shortly to use this knowledge in one of the most hazardous experiences of his life.

They were now, thanks to their treaty, both dry clad in the field-gray uniforms of the German rank and file; and though they felt somewhat strange in these habiliments they enjoyed a feeling of security, especially in view of the populated district they must pass through.

Of the purposes and fate of their late "enemies" they had no inkling and they did not greatly concern themselves about this pair of fugitives who had crossed their path. They knew, from the gossip in "Slops" prison, that Germany was full of deserters who were continually being rounded up because, as Archer blithely put it, they were "punk scouts and had no resourrce - or whatever you call it." Tom did not altogether relish the implication that a deserter might be a good scout or *vice versa*, but he agreed with Archer that the pair they had encountered would probably not "get away with it."

"If they had a couple o' generrals to map it out forr 'em, maybe they would," said Archer.

"I think I'm above you in rank," said Tom, glancing at an arrow sewn on his sleeve.

"I'm hanged if I know what that means," Archer answered. "Therre's a couple morre of 'em on your collarr. Maybe you'rre a generral, hey? I'm just a plain, everyday botch."

"Boche," said Tom.

"Same thing."

They landed at an embankment where a railroad skirted the shore and it occurred to Tom now that the guiding light which had forsaken him the night before was a railroad signal which had been turned the other way after the passage of the train he had heard. At his suggestion, Archer bored a hole in the boat and together they gave it a smart push out into the river.

"Davy Jones forr you, you bloomin' tattle*tile*, as the Tommies would say," Archer observed in reminiscence of his vast and varied acquaintanceship. "Come on now, we've got to join our regiment and blow up a few hospitals. How do you like being a botch, anyway?"

"I'd rather be one now than a year from now," said Tom.

"Thou neverr spakst a truerr worrd.

"Oh, Fritzie Hun, he had a gun,
And other things that's worrse;
He didn't like the foe to strike,
So he shot a Red Cross nurrse,"

Archer rattled on.

"Can't you say *nurse?*" said Tom.

"Surre I can - nurrrrse."

Tom laughed.

They tramped up through the main street of a village, for the populated area was too extensive to afford hope of a reasonably short detour. The few people whom they passed in the darkness paid no particular heed to them. They might have been a couple of khaki-clad boys in America for all the curiosity they excited.

At the railroad station an army officer glared at them when they saluted and seemed on the point of accosting them, which gave them a momentary scare.

"We'd better be careful," said Tom.

"Gee, I thought we had to salute," Archer answered.

They followed the railroad tracks through an open sparsely populated region as far as the small town of Ottersweier. The few persons who were abroad paid no particular attention to them, and as long as no one spoke to them they felt safe, for the street was in almost total darkness. Once a formidable-looking German policeman scrutinized them, or so they thought, and a group of soldiers who were sitting in the dark entrance of a little beer garden looked at them curiously before saluting. Most of these men were crippled, and indeed as they passed along it seemed to the fugitives that nearly every man they passed either had his arm in a sling or was using crutches.

"Do you think maybe they had a hunch we werren't Gerrman soldierrs at all?" Archer queried.

"No," said Tom. "I think they just didn't want to salute us till they were sure we were soldiers like themselves. I think a soldier hasn't got a right even to salute an officer here unless the officer takes some notice of him. Maybe the officer's got to glance at him first, or something."

"G-o-od *night!*" said Archer. "Reminds you of America, don't it - *not 'arf,* as the Tommies say. Wouldn't it seem funny not daring to speak to an officerr therre? Many's the chat I've had with French generals and English ones, too. Didn't I give old Marshal What's-his-name an elastic band to put around his paperrs?"

In all probability he had, for he was an aggressive and brazen youngster without much respect for dignity and authority, and Tom was glad when they reached the hills, for he had been apprehensive lest his comrade might essay a familiar pleasantry with some grim official or launch himself into the perilous pastime of swapping souvenirs with a German soldier.

But they were both to remember this business about saluting which, if Tom was right, was eloquent of the German military system, showing how high was the officer and how low the soldier who might not even pay his arrogant superior the tribute of a salute without permission.

This knowledge was to serve Tom in good stead before many days should pass.

# CHAPTER XXV

## TOM IN WONDERLAND

All through that night, with their compass as a guide, they climbed the hills, keeping in a southerly direction, but verging slightly eastward. In the morning they found themselves on the edge of a high, deeply wooded plateau, which they knew extended with more or less uniformity to the Swiss frontier.

Looking ahead of them, in a southerly direction, they could see dim, solemn aisles of sombre fir trees and the ground was like a brown velvet carpet, yielding gently under their feet. The air was laden with a pungent odor, accentuated by the recent storm, and the damp, resiny fragrance was like a bracing tonic to the fugitives, bidding them welcome to these silent, unfrequented depths.

They were now, indeed, within the precincts of the renowned Schwarzwald, whose wilderness toyland sends forth out of its sequestered hamlets (or did) wooden lions, tigers and rhinoceroses for the whole world, and monkeys on sticks and jumping-jacks and little wooden villages, like the little wooden villages where they are made.

The west slopes of this romantic region were abrupt, almost like the Palisades of the Hudson, running close to the river in some places, and in other places descending several miles back from the shore, so that a panoramic view of southern Alsace was always obtainable from the sharp edge of this forest workshop of Santa Claus. In the east the plateau slopes away and peters out in the lowlands, so that, as one might say, the Black Forest forms a kind of huge natural springboard to afford one a good running jump across the Rhine into Alsace.

Archer's battered and misused geography had not lied about the commissary department of this storied wilderness, for the wild grapes (of which the famous Rhenish wine is made) did indeed grow in "furious what-d'you-call-'ems" or luxurious profusion if you prefer, upon the precipitous western slopes.

All that day they tramped southward, meeting not a soul, and feeling almost as if they were in a church. It seemed altogether grotesque that Germany, grim, fighting, war-crazy Germany, should own such a peaceful region as this.

In the course of the day, they helped the prohibition movement, as Archer said, by eating grapes in such quantities as seriously to reduce the output of Rhenish wine. "But, oh, Ebeneezerr!" he added. "What wouldn't I give for a good russet apple and a dipper of sweet cider."

"You're always thinking about apples and souvenirs," said Tom.

"You can bet I'm going to get a souveneerr in herre, all right!" Archer announced. "Therre ought to be lots of good ones herre, hey?"

"Maybe they grow in furious what-d'you-call-'ems?" suggested sober Tom.

"If it keeps as level as this, we ought to be able to waltz into the barrbed wirre by tomorrow night. This is the only thing about Gerrmany that's on the level, hey?"

Toward evening they had the lesser of the two surprises which were in store for them in the Black Forest. They were hiking along when suddenly Tom paused and listened intently.

"What is it?" Archer asked.

"A bird," said Tom, "but I never heard a bird make a noise like that before."

"He's chirrping in Gerrman," suggested Archer.

The more Tom listened, the more puzzled he became, for he had the scout's familiarity with bird voices and this was a new one to him.

"Therre's a house," Archer said.

And sure enough there, nestling among the firs some distance ahead, was the quaintest little house the boys had ever seen. It was almost like a toy house with a picturesque roof ten sizes too big for it, and a funny little man in a smock sitting in the doorway. Hanging outside was a large cuckoo clock and it was the wooden cuckoo which Tom had heard.

Shavings littered the ground about this tiny, wilderness manufactory, and upon a rough board, like a scout messboard, were a number of little handmade windmills revolving furiously. Wooden soldiers and stolid-looking horses with conventional tails, all fresh from the deft and cunning hands which wielded the harmless jack-knife, were piled helter-skelter in a big basket waiting, waiting, waiting, for the end of the war, to go forth in peace and goodwill to the ends of the earth and nestle snugly in the bottom of Christmas stockings.

This quaint old man could speak scarcely any English, but when the boys made out that he was Swiss, and apparently kindly disposed, they sprawled on the ground and rested, succeeding by dint of motions and a few words of German in establishing a kind of intercourse with him. He was apparently as far removed from the war as if he had lived in the Fiji Islands, and the fugitives felt quite as safe at his rustic abode as if they had been on the planet Mars. His nationality, too, gave them the cheering assurance that they were approaching the frontier.

"Vagons - noh," he said; "no mohr." Then he pointed to his brimming basket and said more which they could not understand.

Like most persons who live in the forest, he seemed neither surprised at their coming nor curious. They gathered that in former days wagons had wound through these forest ways gathering the handiwork of the people, but that they came no more. To Tom it seemed a pathetic thing that Kaiser Bill should reach out his bloody hand and blight the peaceful occupation of this quaint little old man of the forest. Perhaps he would die, far away there in his tree-embowered cottage, before the wagons ever came again, and the overflowing basket would rot away and the windmills blow themselves to pieces....

Percy Keese Fitzhugh

# CHAPTER XXVI

## MAGIC

Leaving the home of the Swiss toymaker, who had shared his simple fare with them, they started southward through the deep wilderness.

Tom's idea was to keep well within the forest, but within access to its western edge, so that they might scan the country across the river at intervals. They were so refreshed and encouraged as they tramped through the deep, unpeopled wilderness which they knew must bring them to the border, and so eager to bring their long journey to an end, that they kept on for a while in the darkness until, to their great surprise, they came upon a sheet of water the bank of which extended as far east and west as they could see. Tom fancied he could just distinguish the dark trees outlined on the opposite shore.

"Let's follow the shore a ways and see if we can get round it," he said.

But a tramp along the edge, first east, then west, brought no general turn in the shore-line and they began to wonder if the Schwarzwald could be bisected by some majestic river.

"I don't think a river so high up would be so wide," Tom said. "If I was sure about that being the other shore over there, we could swim across."

"It would be betterr to get around if we could," said Archer, "because if we'rre goin' wherre people arre we don't want our uniforms all soaked."

"I'm not going to try to find *her*, if that's what you mean," said Tom; "not unless you say so too, anyway."

"What d'you s'pose I dived forr that glass forr?" Archer retorted. "We're goin' to find that girrl - or perish in the attempt - like old What's-his-name. You've got the right idea, Slady."

"It ain't an idea," said Tom soberly, "and if you think it's - kind of - that I - that I - like her -"

"Surre it ain't, it's 'cause you hate herr," said Archer readily.

"You make me tired," said Tom, flushing.

Since they had to sleep somewhere, they decided to bivouac on the shore of this water and take their bearings in the morning. As the night was warm, they took off their coats and hanging them to a spreading branch above them they sprawled upon the cushiony ground, abandoning for once their rule of continuous watch, and were soon fast asleep. You do not need any sleeping powders in the Black Forest, for the soft magic of its resiny air will lull you to repose.

When they awakened in the morning they squirmed with complicated gymnastic yawns, and lay gazing in lazy half slumber into the branches above them. Suddenly Archer jumped to his feet.

"Wherre arre ourr coats?" he cried.

Tom sat up, rubbed his eyes and gazed about. There were no coats to be seen.

"What d'you know about that?" said Archer. "Maybe they

blew away," he added, looking about.

"There hasn't been any wind," said Tom. "Look at that handkerchief." Near him lay a handkerchief which Archer remembered spreading on the ground beside him the night before.

"Well - I'll - be - jiggered," he exclaimed, looking about again in dismay. "Somebody's been herre," he added conclusively.

Tom fell to scrutinizing the ground for footprints, but there was no sign of any and he too gazed about him in bewilderment.

"They didn't walk away, that's sure," he said, "and they didn't blow away either. There wasn't even a breeze."

A thorough search of the immediate locality confirmed their feeling of certainty that the coats had not blown away. Indeed, they could not have blown far even if there had been any wind, for the closeness of the trees to one another would have prevented this. Tom gazed about, then looked at his companion, utterly dumfounded.

"Maybe they blew into the waterr," Archer suggested. But Tom only shook his head and pointed to the light handkerchief upon the ground. A mere breath would have carried that away.

They could only stand and stare at each other. Some one had evidently taken their coats away in the night.

"It's Gerrman efficiency, that's what it is," said Archer.

"Why didn't they take us, too?" Tom asked.

"They'll be along forr us pretty soon," Archer reassured him. "They'rre superrmen - that's what they arre. - Maybe it's some kind of strategy, hey? They can do spooky things, those Huns.

They've got magic uniforms."

"I don't see any reason for it," said sober Tom, still looking about, unable to conquer his amazement.

"That's just it," said Archer. "They do things therre ain't any reason forr just to practice theirr efficiency. Pretty soon you'll see all the allied soldierrs'll be losing their coats. Go-o-o-o-d *night*!"

"Well, I can't find any footprints, that's sure," said Tom, rather chagrined. "I usually can."

"Maybe it was some sort of an airship," Archer suggested.

Whatever the explanation of this extraordinary thing, the coats were gone. There were no footprints, and there had been no wind. And the mysterious affair left the boys aghast.

"One thing sure - we'd better get away from here quick," said Tom.

"You said it! Ebeneezerr, but this place has got the Catskills and old Rip Van Winkle beat! Come on - quick!"

Tom was not sure that one side of the water was any safer than the other in this emergency, and he was almost too nonplussed to do anything, but surely they were in danger, he felt, and would better be upon their way without the loss of a minute. What troubled him not a little also was that the precious spyglass and the compass were with the missing coats.

They could see now that the water was a long, narrow lake the ends of which were just discernible from the midway position along the shore where they stood, and the opposite shore was perhaps a mile distant.

"Are you game to swim it?" Archer asked.

They felt that this would be easier than the long tramp around and that they would have the advantage while swimming of an extended view and would avoid any danger which might lurk behind the trees.

They had almost reached the opposite shore when Archer sputtered and called out to Tom: "Look, look!"

Tom looked and saw, hanging from a branch on the shore they were nearing, the two missing field gray uniform coats.

This was too much. Speechless with amazement they clambered ashore and walked half fearfully up to their fugitive garments. There was no doubt about it, there were the two coats dangling from a low hanging branch, perfectly dry and in the pockets the spy-glass and the trusty compass. The two boys stared blankly at each other.

"Well - what - do - you - know - about - that?" said Archer.

"They didn't steal anything, anyway," said Tom, half under his breath.

Archer stared at the coats, then peered cautiously about among the trees. Then he faced Tom again, who returned his stare in mute astonishment.

"You don't s'pose we could have swum across in ourr sleep, do you?" said Archer.

Tom shook his head thoughtfully. Could it be that those Huns, those fiends of the air and the ocean depths, those demons who could shoot a gun for seventy miles and rear their yellow heads suddenly up out of the green waters close to the American shore - could it be that they were indeed genii - ghouls of evil, who played fast and loose with poor wanderers in the forest until the moment came for crushing them utterly?

Or could it be that this black wilderness, perched upon its

mountain chain, was indeed the magic toyland of all creation, the home of Santa Claus and -

"Come on," said Archer, "let's not stand herre. B'lieve *me*, I want to get as far away from this place as we can!"

# CHAPTER XXVII

## NONNENMATTWEIHER

But the worst was yet to come. They hurried now, for whatever the cause of this extraordinary incident, they wished to get away from it, and having crossed the lake they paused not to dry their garments but continued southward following the almost obliterated wagon tracks which ran from the shore.

"I wonder how the wagons got across?" said Tom.

"Wings," said Archer solemnly, shaking his head.

In a little while they came to the toymaker's cottage, with the mechanical cuckoo and the windmills and the basket of soldiers and animals and the old Swiss toymaker himself, sitting like a big toy, in the doorway.

"Well - I'll - be -" began Archer.

Tom simply gaped, too perplexed to speak. He had believed that he was something of a woodsman, and he certainly believed that he would not go north supposing that he was going south! Could there be another Swiss toymaker, and another cottage and another squawking cuckoo, exactly like the others? Were they all alike, the lonesome denizens of this spooky place, like the wooden inhabitants of a Noah's ark?

"This Hun forest has got Aladdin's cave beat twenty ways,"

said Archer. "Either we'rre crazy or this place is."

Suddenly the bright thought occurred to Tom to look at his compass. Unless the magnetic pole had changed its position, and the whole earth gone askew, they were tramping northward, as he saw to his unutterable amazement.

"Did we swim across the lake or didn't we?" he demanded of Archer, roused out of his wonted stolidness.

"Surre, we did!"

"Then I give it up," said Tom resignedly. "The compass says north - we're going north. This is the very same toymaker."

"Go-o-od *night!*" said Archer, with even more than his usual vehemence. "Maybe the Gerrmans have conquerred the Norrth Pole and taken all the steel to make mountains, just like they knocked international law all endways, hey? That's why the compass don't point right. G-o-o-o-o-od *night!*"

This ingenious theory, involving a rather large piece of strategy even for "supermen," did not appeal to Tom's sober mind.

"That's what it is," said Archer. "You've got to admit that if they could send Zeps and submarines and things to the North Pole and cop all the steel, the British navy, and ourrs too, would be floppin' around the ocean like a chicken with its head cut off. - It's a good idea!"

Tom went up to the old toymaker, who greeted them with a smile, seeming no more surprised to see them than he had been the day before.

"North - *north?*" asked Tom, pointing.

"Nort - yah," said the old man, pointing too.

"Water," said Tom; "swim - *swim* across" (he pointed

Percy Keese Fitzhugh

southward and made the motions of swimming). The old man nodded as if he understood.

"Ach - vauder, yach, - Nonnenmattweiher."

"What?" said Tom.

"*What?*" said Archer.

"Nonnenmattweiher," said the old man. "Yah."

"He wants to know what's the matter with you," said Archer.

"Water," Tom repeated, almost in desperation.

"Swim (he went through the motions): Swim across water to south - start south, go north." He made no attempt to convey the incident of the vanishing coats.

"Water - yah, - Nonnenmattweiher," the man repeated.

At last, by dint of repeating words and swinging their arms and going through a variety of extraordinary motions, the boys succeeded in conveying to the little man that something was wrong in the neighborhood of the lake, and he appeared willing enough to go back with them, trotting along beside Tom in his funny belted blouse, for all the world like a mechanical toy. Tom had his misgivings as to whether they would really reach the lake no matter which way they went, but they did reach it, and standing under the tree where they had recovered their vanished coats they tried to explain to the old man what had happened - that they had crossed from the north to the south bank and continued southward, only to find that they were going north!

Suddenly a new light illumined the little man's countenance and he chuckled audibly. Then he pointed across the lake, chattering and chuckling the while, and went through a series of strange motions, spreading his legs farther and farther apart, pointing to the ground between them, and concluded this exhibition with a sweeping motion of his hands as if bidding some invisible presence of that enchanted place God-speed across the water.

"Och - goo," he said, and shook his head and laughed.

"I know what he means," said Tom at last, with undisguised chagrin, "and I'm a punk scout. I didn't notice anything at all. Come on. We've got to swim across again - that's south, all right."

"What is it?" asked Archer.

"I'll show you when we get there - come on."

The little Swiss toymaker stood watching them and laughing with a spasmodic laugh which he might have caught from his own wooden cuckoo. When they reached the other shore Tom fell at once to examining a very perceptible rift in the earth a few feet from the shore.

"Do you see?" he said, "we floated over on this piece of land. The tree where we hung our coats was on the *real* shore, and -"

"Go-od night, and it missed the boat," concluded Archer.

"This tree here is something like it," said Tom, "and that's where I made my mistake. I ought to have noticed the trees and I ought to have noticed the crack. Gee, if my scout patrol ever heard of that! 'Specially Roy Blakeley," he added, shaking his head dubiously.

It was indeed something of a "bull" in scouting, though perhaps a more experienced forester than Tom would have become as confused as he in the same circumstances. Perhaps if he had been as companionable with his school geography as Archer had been with his he might have known about the famous Lake Nonnenmattweiher in the silent depths of the

Schwarzwald and of its world-famed floating island, which makes its nocturnal cruises from shore to shore, a silent, restless voyager on that black pine-embowered lake.

As the boys looked back across the water they could see the little Swiss toymaker still standing upon the shore, and looking at him through the rescued glass (of which they were soon to make better use), Tom could see that his odd little figure was shaking with merriment - as if he were wound up.

# CHAPTER XXVIII

## AN INVESTMENT

Often, in the grim, bloody days to come, they thought of the little Swiss toymaker up there among his windmills and Noah's arks, and of his laugh at their expense. A merry little gnome he was, the very spirit of the Black Forest.

Their last sight of him marked almost the end of their wanderings. For another day's tramping through the solemn depths brought them to a little community, a tiny forest village, made up of just such cottages and people, and they made a detour to avoid it, only to run plunk into another miniature industrial centre which they also "side-stepped," though indeed the iron fist seemed not to be very tightly closed upon these primitive knights of the jack-knife and chisel; and they saw no dreaded sign of authority.

Still they did not wish to be reckless and when they sought food and shelter it was at a sequestered cottage several miles from the nearest habitation. Here Tom showed his button but the old man (they saw no young men) seemed not to know what it meant, although he gave them food, apparently believing them to be German soldiers.

Tom believed that they must have journeyed fifty or sixty miles southward, verging away from the river so as to keep within the depths of the forest, and he realized that the time had come for them to consider just what course they were going to pursue.

"If we're going to try to find her," he said rather hesitatingly, "we ought to hit it west so's we can take a pike across the river. But if we keep straight south we'll strike the river after it bends, if that old weaver knew what he was talking about, and when we cross it we'll be in Switzerland. We'll do whatever you say. Going straight south would be easier and safer," he added, with his usual blunt honesty; "and if we cross back into Alsace we'll have to go past houses and people and we'll be taking chances. - I admit it's like things in a book - I mean rescuing girls," he said, with his characteristic awkward frankness, "and maybe some people would say it was crazy, kind of -" What he meant was *romantic*, but he didn't exactly know how to say that. "As long as we've been lucky so far maybe we ought to get across the frontier and over to France as quick as we can. I s'pose that's where we belong - most of all -"

"Is that what you think?" said Archer.

"I ain't sayin' what I think, but -"

"Well, then, I'll say what *I* think," retorted Archer. "You're always telling about thoughts you've had. I don't claim I'm as good as you arre at having thoughts, but if therre's a soldierr wounded they send two or three soldierrs to carry the stretcherr, don't they? Maybe those soldierrs ought to be fighting, but saving a person comes firrst. You've hearrd about giving all you have to the Red Cross. All *we* got is the *chance* to get away. We've got morre chance than we had when we starrted, 'cause you'rre a good scout -"

"I don't claim -"

"Shut up," said Archer; "so it's like saving up ourr chances and adding to 'em, till now we're 'most in Switzerland and we got a good big chance saved up. I'll tell you what I'm going to do with mine - I'm going to give it to the Red Cross - *kind of* - as you'd say. If that girrl is worrkin' on that road and I can find herr, I'm goin' to. If I get pinched, all right. So it ain't a question of what *we'rre* goin' to do; it's a question of: Are *you* with me? You're always tellin' when yourr thoughts come to you. Well, I got that one just before I dived for the glass. So that's the way I'm going to invest *my* chance, 'cause I haven't got anything else to give.... I heard in prison about the Liberty Bond buttons they give you to wearr back home. I'd like to have one of those blamed things to wearr for a souveneerr."

Tom Slade had stood silent throughout this harangue, and now he laughed a little awkwardly. "It's better than investing money," he said, "and what I'm laughing at - kind of," he added with infinite relief and satisfaction showing through the emotion he was trying to repress; "what I'm laughing at is how you're always thinking about souvenirs."

*   *   *   *   *

So it was decided that their little joint store, their savings, as one might say - their standing capital of *chance* which they had improved and added to - should be invested in the hazardous business of rescuing a daughter of France from her German captors. It was *giving* with a vengeance.

It is a pity that there was no button to signalize this kind of a contribution.

# CHAPTER XXIX

## CAMOUFLAGE

They turned westward now in a direction which Tom thought would bring them about opposite the Alsatian town of Norne. A day's journey took them out of the forest proper into a rocky region of sparse vegetation from which they could see the river winding ribbonlike in the distance. Beyond it in the flat Alsatian country lay a considerable city which, from what old Melotte had told them, they believed to be Mulhausen.

"Norne is a little to the south of that and closer to the river," said Tom.

They picked their way along the edge of the palisades, concealing themselves among the rocks, and as they thus worked to the southward the precipitous heights and the river converged until they were almost directly above the water. At last, looking down, they saw upon the narrow strip of shore directly below them the old castle of which Melotte had told them. There was no other in sight. From their dizzy perch among the concealing rocks they could see almost the whole width of southern Alsace in panorama, as one sees New York from the Palisades of the Hudson, and in the distance the dim outlines of the Vosges mountains, beyond which lay France.

Not far from the river on the Alsatian side and (as old Melotte had said) directly opposite the castle, was a small town which Tom studied carefully with the glass.

"That's it," he said, relieved, for both of them had harbored a lingering fear that these places existed only in the childish mind of the blue-eyed old weaver. "Melotte was right," he added. "Wait a minute - I'll let you look. You can see the new road and people working on it and - wait a minute - I can see a little flag on one house."

There was no doubt about it. There was the town of Norne, and just west of it a road with tiny figures distributed along it.

Archer was all a-quiver as he took the glass. "I can see the house," he said; "it's right near the road, it's got a flag on it. When the light strikes it you can see the black spot. Oh, look, look!"

"I can't look when you've got the glass," said Tom in his dull way.

"I can see the battleline!" cried Archer.

Tom took the glass with unusual excitement. Far across the Alsatian country, north and south, ran a dim, gray line, seeming to have no more substance than a rainbow or the dust in a sun-ray. Far to the north it bent westward and he knew its course lay through the mountains. But short of those blue heights it seemed to peter out in a sort of gray mist. And that was all that could be seen of that seething, bloody line where the destinies of mankind were being contended for.

It was easy for the boys to imagine that the specks they could see were soldiers, American soldiers perhaps, and that low-hung clouds were the smoke of thundering artillery....

"I wonder if we'll ever get over there," said Archer.

"Over there," Tom repeated abstractedly.

\* \* \* \* \*

Percy Keese Fitzhugh

Their program now must be one of stealth, not boldness, and they did not wish to be seen scrambling down the heights in broad daylight; so they waited for the night, regaling themselves out of the "furious profusion" of grapes of which there seemed enough to make an ocean of Rhenish wine.

It was dark when they reached the river bank and explored the shore for some means of getting across. At last they discovered a float with several boats attached to it and a ramshackle structure hard by within which was a light and the familiar sound of a baby crying.

"We've got to make up our minds not to be scared," said Tom, "and we mustn't *look* as if we were scared. You can't make believe you're not scared if you are. Let's try to make ourselves think we're really German soldiers and then other people will think so. We've got to act just like 'em."

"If you mean we've got to murrderr that baby," said Archer; "no sirree! Not for mine!"

"That *ain't* what I mean," said Tom. "You know Jeb Rushmore at Temple Camp? He came from Arizona. He says you can always tell a fake cowboy no matter how he may be dressed up because he don't *feel* like the West. It ain't just the uniforms that do it; it's the way we *act.*"

"I get you," said Archer.

"I wouldn't do the things they do any more than I have to," Tom said; "and I don't know exactly how they feel -"

"They don't feel at all," interrupted Archer.

"But if we act as if we didn't care and ain't afraid, we stand a chance."

"We've got to act as if we owned the earrth," Archer agreed.

"Except if we should meet an officer," Tom concluded.

In his crude way Tom had stumbled upon a great truth, which is the one chief consideration in the matter of successful disguise. *You must feel your part if you would act it.* As he had said, they did not know how German soldiers felt (no civilized mortal knows that!), but he knew that the Germans were plentiful hereabouts and no novelty, and that their only hope of simulating two of them lay in banishing all timidity and putting on a bold front.

"One thing, we've got to keep our mouths shut," he said. "Most people won't bother us but we've got to look out for officers. I'm going to tear my shirt and make a sling for my arm and you've got to limp - and keep your mind on it. When you're faking, you limp with your brain - remember."

The first test of their policy was successful beyond their fondest dreams, though their parts were not altogether agreeable to them. They marched down to the float, unfastened one of the boats with a good deal of accompanying noise and started out into the river, just as Kaiser Bill had started across Belgium. A woman with a baby in her arms appeared in the doorway and stared at them - then banged the door shut.

They were greatly elated at their success and considered the taking of the boat as a war measure, as probably the poor German woman did too.

Once upon the other side they walked boldly into the considerable town of Norne and over the first paved streets which they had seen in many a day. They did not get out of the way of people at all; they let the people scurry out of *their* way and were very bold and high and mighty and unmannerly, and truly German in all the nice little particulars which make the German such an unspeakable beast.

Tom forgot all about the good old scout rule to do a good turn every day and camouflaged his manners by doing a bad turn every minute - or as nearly that as possible. It was good camouflage, and got them safely through the streets of Norne, where they must do considerable hunting to find the home of old Melotte's friend Blondel. They finally located it on the outskirts of the town and recognized it by the billet flag which Melotte had described to them.

# CHAPTER XXX

## THE SPIRIT OF FRANCE

It was the success of their policy of boldness, together with something which Madame Blondel told him, which prompted Tom to undertake the impudent and daring enterprise which was later to make him famous on the western front.

Blondel himself, notwithstanding his sixty-five years, had been pressed into military service, but Madame Blondel remained in the little house on the edge of the town in calm disregard of the German officers who had turned her little home into a headquarters while the new road was being made. For this, of course, was being done under the grim eye of the Military.

The havoc wrought by these little despots, minions of the great despot, in the simple abode of the poor old French couple, was eloquent of the whole Prussian system.

The officer whose heroic duty it was to oversee the women and girls slaving with pick and shovel had turned the little abode out of windows, to make it comfortable for himself and his guests, treating the furniture and all the little household gods with the same disdainful brutality that his masters had shown for Louvain Cathedral. The German instinct is always the same, whether it be on a small or a large scale - whether kicking furniture or blowing up hospitals.

Amid the ruins of her tidy little home, Madame Blondel

lingered in undaunted proprietorship - the very spirit of gallant, indomitable France!

Perhaps, too, the bold entrance into these tyrant-ridden premises of the two American boys under the forbidding flag of Teuton authority, had something in it of the spirit of America. At least so Madame Blondel seemed to regard it; and when Tom showed her his little button she threw her arms around him, extending the area of her assault to Archer as well.

"*Vive l'Amerique!*" she cried, with a fine look of defiance in her snapping eyes.

She took the boys upstairs to a room - the only one, apparently, which she could call her own - and here they told her their story.

It appeared that for many years she had lived in America, where her husband had worked in a silk mill and she had kept a little road-house, tempting American autoists with French cooking and wine of Burgundy. She spoke English very well, save for a few charming little slips and notwithstanding that she was short and stout and wore spectacles, she was over-flowing with the spirit of her beloved country, and with a weakness for adventure and romance which took Tom and Archer by storm. A true Frenchwoman indeed, defying with a noble heroism Time and Circumstance and vulgar trespasses under her very roof.

"So you will rescue Mam'selle," she said clasping her hands and pressing them to her breast with an inspiring look in her eyes. "So! This is America - how you say - in a nutshell. Yess?"

"It seems to me you're France in a nutshell," said Tom awkwardly, "and downstairs it's Germany in a nutshell."

"Ah-h-h!" She gave a fine shrug of disgust; "*he* have gone to Berlin. Tomorrow night late, his comrade will come - tomorrow night. So you are safe. And you are ze true knight -

so! You will r-rescue Mam'selle," and she placed her two hands on Tom's shoulders, looking at him with delight, and ended by embracing him.

She seemed more interested in his rescuing "Mam'selle" than in anything else and that apparently because it was a bold adventure in gallantry. A true Frenchwoman indeed.

"She'd make a bully scoutmaster," Tom whispered to Archer.

"They might as well try to capturre the moon as put France out of business," said Archer.

Yes, big or little, man or woman, one or a million, in devastated home or devastated country, she is always the same, gallant, spirited, defiant. *Vive la France!*

While Madame Blondel plied them with food she told them the story of the new road - another shameless item in the wake of German criminality and dishonor.

"They will wait to see if Amerique can send her troops. They will trust zese submarines - so long. No more! All the while they make zis road - ozzer roads. Zere will be ze tramping of zese *beasts* over zese roads to little Switzerland yet!" she said, falling into the French manner in her anger. "So zey will stab her in ze back! Ug-g-g-gh!"

"Do you think that Florette and her mother are both there?" Tom asked.

"Ah," she said slyly; "you wish not that her mother should be there? So you will be ze true knight! Ah, you are a bad boy!"

To Tom's embarrassment she embraced him again, by way of showing that she was not altogether averse to bad boys.

"That ain't the way it is at all," he said flashing awkwardly. "I want to save 'em both. That's the only thing I'm thinking about."

"Ah," she laughed slyly, to Archer's delight. "You are a bad boy! Iss he not a bad boy? Yess?" She turned upon Archer. "Sixty years old I am, but still would I have so much happiness to be ze boy. See! Blondel and I, we run away to our marriage so many years ago. No one can catch us. So! Ziss is ze way - yess? Am I right?" She pointed her finger at poor Tom. "Ah, you are ze true knight! Even yet, maybe, you will fight ze duel - so! Listen! I will tell you how you will trrick ze Prussians."

This was getting down to business and much to Tom's relief though Archer had enjoyed the little scene hugely.

"See," she said more soberly. "I will tell you. Every young mam'selle must work - all are there. From north and south have they brought them. All! But not our older women. Like soldiers they must obey. Here to this very house come those that rebel - arrest! Some are sent back with - what you say? Reprimand. Some to prison. I cannot speak. My own countrywomen! Ug-gh! Zese wretches!"

"So now I shall see if you are true Americans." She looked straight at Tom, and even her homely spectacles did not detract from the fire that burned in her eyes. Here was a woman, who if she had but been a man, could have done anything. "I shall give you ze paper - all print. Ze warrant. You see?" She paused, throwing her head back with such a fine air of defiance that even her wrinkled face and homely domestic garb could not dim its glory. "*You shall arrest Mam'selle!* Here you shall bring her. See - listen! You know what our great Napoleon say? 'Across ze Alps lies Italee.' So shall you arrest Mam'selle!" She put her arm on Tom's shoulder and looked into his eyes with a kind of inspiring frenzy. "Close, so very close," she whispered significantly, "*across ze Rhine lies Switzerland*!"

# CHAPTER XXXI

## THE END OF THE TRAIL

Not in all the far-flung battleline was there a more pitiable sight than the bright sun beheld as he poured his stifling rays down upon the winding line of upturned earth which lay in fresh piles across the country of southern Alsace.

Almost to the Swiss border it ran, but no one could get across the Swiss border here without running into Prussian bayonets. To the east, where the Rhine flowed and where the mountains were, some reckless soul might manage it in a night's journeying, if he would brave the lonesome fastnesses; though even there the meshes of forbidding wire, charged with a death-giving voltage, stretched across the path. It was not an inviting route.

You may believe it or not, as you please, but along this new road score upon score of young women and mere girls toiled and slaved with pickaxe and shovel. And some fell and were lifted up again, with threats and imprecations, and toiled on. There were some who came from Belgium, whose hands had been cut off, and these were harnessed and drew stones. They lived, if you call it living, in tents and wooden barracks along the line of work, and in these they spent their few hours of respite in fearful, restless slumber.

Over them, like a black and threatening cloud, was the clenched, blood-wet iron fist. Now and then one broke down in hysterics and was "arrested" and taken before the commander who sprawled and drank wine in a peasant cottage nearby. For the road must be made and German militarism tolerates no nonsense....

Across the fields toward this road passed a young fellow in the uniform of a petty officer. He carried in his hand a paper and a pair of handcuffs. He was repeating to himself a phrase in the German language in which he had just been carefully drilled. "Wo ist sie?"

It was all the German that he knew.

Approaching the road, he passed along among the workers, who glanced up at him covertly and plied their implements a little harder for his presence. Coming upon a soldier who was marching back and forth on guard, the officer showed him the paper and said, "*Wo ist sie?*" The guard pointed farther down the line at another soldier, whom the officer approached and addressed with his one, newly-learned question. The second soldier scanned the workers under his charge, then made as if to take the paper and the handcuffs, but the officer held them from him with true German arrogance, intimating that all he wished was to have the worker identified and he would do the rest. He did not deign to speak to the soldier.

When the subject of his quest had been pointed out to him he strode over to her, with a motion of his hand bidding the soldier remain at his post. The girls, who were working ankle-deep in the thick earth, fell back as this grim embodiment of authority passed and stole fearful glances at him as he laid his hand upon the shoulder of one of their number who was throwing stones out of the roadway. She was a slender girl, almost too delicate for housework, one would have said, and her face bore an expression of utter listlessness - the listlessness that comes from long fatigue and lost hope. Her eyes had the startled, terror-stricken look of a frightened animal as she looked up into the face of the young officer.

"Don't speak and don't look surprised," he said in an undertone, as he snapped the handcuffs on her wrists. "I'm Tom Slade - don't you remember? You have to come with me and we'll take you across the Swiss border tonight. It's all planned. Don't talk and don't be scared. Answer low - Is your mother here?"

A heavy stone that she was holding fell and he could feel her shoulder trembling under his hand. She looked at him in doubtful recognition, for the face was grim and cold and there was a look of hard steel in the eyes. Then she glanced in terror at one of the soldiers who was marching back and forth, rifle in hand.

"He won't interfere - he won't even dare to salute me. If he comes near I'll knock him down. Is your mother here?"

"She iss wiz ze friends in Leteur. Her zey do not take."

Her voice was low and full of a terror which she seemed unable to overcome and as she looked fearfully about Tom was reminded of the night when they had talked together alone in the arbor.

"They didn't catch me yet and they won't," he said. "They're not scouts. Come on."

She followed him out of the upturned earth and down the line, where he strode like a lord of creation. Never so much as a glance did he deign to give a soldier. A few of the young women who dared to look up watched the two as they cut across a field and, whispering, some said her lot would be worse than she suspected - that her arrest was only a ruse.... They came nearer to the truth in that than they knew.

Others spoke enviously, saying that, whatever befell her, at least she would have a little rest. The more bold among them continued to steal covert glances as the two went across the field, and fell to work again with a better submission, noticing the overbearing demeanor of the brutal young officer who had arrested their companion.

"You are come again," she finally said timidly; "like ze good genii." It was difficult for her to speak, but Tom was willing for her to cry and seem agitated, for they were coming to houses now, where crippled soldiers sat about and children scurried, frightened, out of their path and called their mothers who came out to stare.

"My father - I may not yet talk -"

"Yes, you can talk now. I know all about it."

"Everything you know - you are wonderful. He told us how ze zheneral, he say, '*Lafayette, we are here!*' And now you are here -"

"I told you you could sing the *Marseillaise* again," he said simply. "When we get over there, you can."

"You have come before zem, even," she said, her voice breaking with emotion. "I cannot speak, you see, but some day ze Americans, zey will be here, and you are here ze first -"

"Don't try to talk," he said huskily. "Over in America we have girl scouts - kind of. They call 'em Camp Fire Girls. Some people make fun of 'em, but they can climb and they don't scream when they get in a boat, and they ain't afraid of the woods, and they don't care if it rains, and they ain't a-scared of noises, and all like that. You got to be one of them tonight. You got to be just like a feller - kind of. Even if you're tired you got to stick it out - just like France is doing."

"I am ze daughter of France," she said proudly, catching his meaning, "and you have come like America. Before, in Leteur, I was afraid. No more am I afraid. I will be ziss fiery camp girl - so!"

"Not fiery camp girl," said Tom dully; "Camp Fire Girl."

"So! I will be zat!"

"And tomorrow we'll be in Switzerland. And soon as we get across I'm going to make you sing the *Marseillaise*, so's when I get to Frenchy - Armand - I can tell him you sang it and nobody stopped you. You remember the other feller that was with me. He says we're going to take you to Armand as a souvenir. That's what he's always talking about - souvenirs."

*   *   *   *   *

It did not occupy much space in the American newspapers for there were more important things to relate. The English were circling around some ridge or other; the French were straightening out a salient, and the Germans had failed to surprise the Americans near Arracourt. The American airmen got the credit for that.

So there was only a brief account. "Two American Ship's Boys Reach France," heading said, and then followed this summary narrative as sent out by the Associated Press:

"Two American boys are reported to have reached General Pershing's forces in France, having escaped from a German prison camp and passed the Swiss frontier at an unfrequented spot after picking their way through the wilder section of the Black Forest in Baden. They subsisted chiefly on roots and grapes. Both are said to have been in the U.S. Transport Service. A despatch from Basel says that the Red Cross authorities are caring for a French Alsatian girl whom the fugitives rescued from German servitude by impersonating German military authorities. The details of their exploit are not given in the despatches.

"The American Y. M. C. A. at Nancy has no knowledge of such a girl being brought across the border and doubts the truth of this story, saying that such a rescue would be quite impossible. Another account says that the two boys upon reaching the American troops, notified a brother of the girl who was training with the expeditionary forces and that this brother was given a furlough to visit Molin, just below the Swiss frontier, where the girl was being cared for. This soldier's name is given as Armand Leteur. He is reported to have found his sister in a state of utter collapse from the treatment she had received while toiling on the roads in Alsace. One report has it that her wrist had been branded by a hot iron. The two youngsters are said to have chosen an unfrequented spot where the frontier crosses the mountains and to have manipulated the electrified barbed wire with a pair of rubber gloves which they had found in the wreck of a fallen German airship. The correspondent of the London *Times* says that one of these gloves has been sent to President Wilson by its proud possessor as a souvenir.

"Washington, Oct. 12. - Administration officials here have no knowledge of any rubber glove being received by President Wilson but say that the arrival of two boys, fugitives from Germany, has been officially reported by the military authorities in France and that they brought with them a letter taken from a dead German soldier which contained references to the impending German assault near Arracourt, thus enabling our men to anticipate and confound the Hun plans. Both of the boys, whose names are given as Archibald Slade and Thomas Archer, are now in training behind the American lines. A *Thomas* Slade is reported to have been in the steward's department of the Transport *Montauk* which was struck by a submarine last spring.

"Reuter's Agency confirms the story of the rescue of the girl and of her reunion with her brother."

# Choose from Thousands of 1stWorldLibrary Classics By

A. M. Barnard
Ada Leverson
Adolphus William Ward
Aesop
Agatha Christie
Alexander Aaronsohn
Alexander Kielland
Alexandre Dumas
Alfred Gatty
Alfred Ollivant
Alice Duer Miller
Alice Turner Curtis
Alice Dunbar
Allen Chapman
Ambrose Bierce
Amelia E. Barr
Amory H. Bradford
Andrew Lang
Andrew McFarland Davis
Andy Adams
Anna Alice Chapin
Anna Sewell
Annie Besant
Annie Hamilton Donnell
Annie Payson Call
Annie Roe Carr
Annonaymous
Anton Chekhov
Arnold Bennett
Arthur Conan Doyle
Arthur M. Winfield
Arthur Ransome
Arthur Schnitzler
Atticus
B.H. Baden-Powell
B. M. Bower
B. C. Chatterjee
Baroness Emmuska Orczy
Baroness Orczy
Basil King
Bayard Taylor
Ben Macomber
Bertha Muzzy Bower
Bjornstjerne Bjornson
Booth Tarkington
Boyd Cable
Bram Stoker
C. Collodi
C. E. Orr

C. M. Ingleby
Carolyn Wells
Catherine Parr Traill
Charles A. Eastman
Charles Amory Beach
Charles Dickens
Charles Dudley Warner
Charles Farrar Browne
Charles Ives
Charles Kingsley
Charles Klein
Charles Hanson Towne
Charles Lathrop Pack
Charles Romyn Dake
Charles Whibley
Charles Willing Beale
Charlotte M. Braeme
Charlotte M. Yonge
Charlotte Perkins Stetson
Clair W. Hayes
Clarence Day Jr.
Clarence E. Mulford
Clemence Housman
Confucius
Coningsby Dawson
Cornelis DeWitt Wilcox
Cyril Burleigh
D. H. Lawrence
Daniel Defoe
David Garnett
Dinah Craik
Don Carlos Janes
Donald Keyhoe
Dorothy Kilner
Dougan Clark
Douglas Fairbanks
E. Nesbit
E.P.Roe
E. Phillips Oppenheim
Earl Barnes
Edgar Rice Burroughs
Edith Van Dyne
Edith Wharton
Edward Everett Hale
Edward J. O'Biren
Edward S. Ellis
Edwin L. Arnold
Eleanor Atkins
Eliot Gregory

Elizabeth Gaskell
Elizabeth McCracken
Elizabeth Von Arnim
Ellem Key
Emerson Hough
Emilie F. Carlen
Emily Dickinson
Enid Bagnold
Enilor Macartney Lane
Erasmus W. Jones
Ernie Howard Pie
Ethel May Dell
Ethel Turner
Ethel Watts Mumford
Eugenie Foa
Eugene Wood
Eustace Hale Ball
Evelyn Everett-green
Everard Cotes
F. H. Cheley
F. J. Cross
F. Marion Crawford
Federick Austin Ogg
Ferdinand Ossendowski
Francis Bacon
Francis Darwin
Frances Hodgson Burnett
Frances Parkinson Keyes
Frank Gee Patchin
Frank Harris
Frank Jewett Mather
Frank L. Packard
Frank V. Webster
Frederic Stewart Isham
Frederick Trevor Hill
Frederick Winslow Taylor
Friedrich Kerst
Friedrich Nietzsche
Fyodor Dostoyevsky
G.A. Henty
G.K. Chesterton
Gabrielle E. Jackson
Garrett P. Serviss
Gaston Leroux
George A. Warren
George Ade
Geroge Bernard Shaw
George Durston
George Ebers

George Eliot
George Gissing
George MacDonald
George Meredith
George Orwell
George Sylvester Viereck
George Tucker
George W. Cable
George Wharton James
Gertrude Atherton
Gordon Casserly
Grace E. King
Grace Gallatin
Grace Greenwood
Grant Allen
Guillermo A. Sherwell
Gulielma Zollinger
Gustav Flaubert
H. A. Cody
H. B. Irving
H.C. Bailey
H. G. Wells
H. H. Munro
H. Irving Hancock
H. Rider Haggard
H. W. C. Davis
Haldeman Julius
Hall Caine
Hamilton Wright Mabie
Hans Christian Andersen
Harold Avery
Harold McGrath
Harriet Beecher Stowe
Harry Castlemon
Harry Coghill
Harry Houidini
Hayden Carruth
Helent Hunt Jackson
Helen Nicolay
Hendrik Conscience
Hendy David Thoreau
Henri Barbusse
Henrik Ibsen
Henry Adams
Henry Ford
Henry Frost
Henry James
Henry Jones Ford
Henry Seton Merriman
Henry W Longfellow
Herbert A. Giles

Herbert Carter
Herbert N. Casson
Herman Hesse
Hildegard G. Frey
Homer
Honore De Balzac
Horace B. Day
Horace Walpole
Horatio Alger Jr.
Howard Pyle
Howard R. Garis
Hugh Lofting
Hugh Walpole
Humphry Ward
Ian Maclaren
Inez Haynes Gillmore
Irving Bacheller
Isabel Hornibrook
Israel Abrahams
Ivan Turgenev
J.G.Austin
J. Henri Fabre
J. M. Barrie
J. Macdonald Oxley
J. S. Fletcher
J. S. Knowles
J. Storer Clouston
Jack London
Jacob Abbott
James Allen
James Andrews
James Baldwin
James Branch Cabell
James DeMille
James Joyce
James Lane Allen
James Lane Allen
James Oliver Curwood
James Oppenheim
James Otis
James R. Driscoll
Jane Austen
Jane L. Stewart
Janet Aldridge
Jens Peter Jacobsen
Jerome K. Jerome
John Burroughs
John Cournos
John F. Kennedy
John Gay
John Glasworthy

John Habberton
John Joy Bell
John Kendrick Bangs
John Milton
John Philip Sousa
Jonas Lauritz Idemil Lie
Jonathan Swift
Joseph A. Altsheler
Joseph Carey
Joseph Conrad
Joseph E. Badger Jr
Joseph Hergesheimer
Joseph Jacobs
Jules Vernes
Julian Hawthrone
Julie A Lippmann
Justin Huntly McCarthy
Kakuzo Okakura
Kenneth Grahame
Kenneth McGaffey
Kate Langley Bosher
Kate Langley Bosher
Katherine Cecil Thurston
Katherine Stokes
L. A. Abbot
L. T. Meade
L. Frank Baum
Latta Griswold
Laura Dent Crane
Laura Lee Hope
Laurence Housman
Lawrence Beasley
Leo Tolstoy
Leonid Andreyev
Lewis Carroll
Lewis Sperry Chafer
Lilian Bell
Lloyd Osbourne
Louis Hughes
Louis Tracy
Louisa May Alcott
Lucy Fitch Perkins
Lucy Maud Montgomery
Luther Benson
Lydia Miller Middleton
Lyndon Orr
M. Corvus
M. H. Adams
Margaret E. Sangster
Margret Howth
Margaret Vandercook

Margret Penrose
Maria Edgeworth
Maria Thompson Daviess
Mariano Azuela
Marion Polk Angellotti
Mark Overton
Mark Twain
Mary Austin
Mary Catherine Crowley
Mary Cole
Mary Hastings Bradley
Mary Roberts Rinehart
Mary Rowlandson
M. Wollstonecraft Shelley
Maud Lindsay
Max Beerbohm
Myra Kelly
Nathaniel Hawthrone
Nicolo Machiavelli
O. F. Walton
Oscar Wilde
Owen Johnson
P.G. Wodehouse
Paul and Mabel Thorne
Paul G. Tomlinson
Paul Severing
Percy Brebner
Peter B. Kyne
Plato
R. Derby Holmes
R. L. Stevenson
R. S. Ball
Rabindranath Tagore
Rahul Alvares
Ralph Bonehill
Ralph Henry Barbour
Ralph Victor
Ralph Waldo Emmerson
Rene Descartes
Rex Beach

Rex E. Beach
Richard Harding Davis
Richard Jefferies
Richard Le Gallienne
Robert Barr
Robert Frost
Robert Gordon Anderson
Robert L. Drake
Robert Lansing
Robert Lynd
Robert Michael Ballantyne
Robert W. Chambers
Rosa Nouchette Carey
Rudyard Kipling
Samuel B. Allison
Samuel Hopkins Adams
Sarah Bernhardt
Sarah C. Hallowell
Selma Lagerlof
Sherwood Anderson
Sigmund Freud
Standish O'Grady
Stanley Weyman
Stella Benson
Stella M. Francis
Stephen Crane
Stewart Edward White
Stijn Streuvels
Swami Abhedananda
Swami Parmananda
T. S. Ackland
T. S. Arthur
The Princess Der Ling
Thomas A. Janvier
Thomas A Kempis
Thomas Anderton
Thomas Bailey Aldrich
Thomas Bulfinch
Thomas De Quincey
Thomas Dixon

Thomas H. Huxley
Thomas Hardy
Thomas More
Thornton W. Burgess
U. S. Grant
Valentine Williams
Various Authors
Vaughan Kester
Victor Appleton
Victoria Cross
Virginia Woolf
Wadsworth Camp
Walter Camp
Walter Scott
Washington Irving
Wilbur Lawton
Wilkie Collins
Willa Cather
Willard F. Baker
William Dean Howells
William le Queux
W. Makepeace Thackeray
William W. Walter
William Shakespeare
Winston Churchill
Yei Theodora Ozaki
Yogi Ramacharaka
Young E. Allison
Zane Grey

www.ingramcontent.com/pod-product-compliance
Lightning Source LLC
Chambersburg PA
CBHW030755150426
42813CB00068B/3109/J